W9-DEK-681

The Alamo

Other titles in the World History Series

The Alamo

Don Nardo

LUCENT BOOKS

A part of Gale, Cengage Learning

CENGAGE Learning·

Detroit • New York • San Francisco • New Haven, Conn • Waterville, Maine • London

© 2013 Gale, Cengage Learning

LIBRARY OF CONGRESS CATALOGING-IN-PUBLICATION DATA

Nardo, Don, 1947-
The Alamo / by Don Nardo.
  p. cm. -- (World history)
Includes bibliographical references and index.
ISBN 978-1-4205-0861-1 (hardcover)
1. Alamo (San Antonio, Tex.)--Siege, 1836--Juvenile literature. I. Title.
F390.N37 2013
976.4'03--dc23

2012025612

Lucent Books
27500 Drake Rd.
Farmington Hills, MI 48331

ISBN-13: 978-1-4205-0861-1
ISBN-10: 1-4205-0861-X

Printed in the United States of America
1 2 3 4 5 6 7 16 15 14 13 12

Contents

Foreword

Each year, on the first day of school, nearly every history teacher faces the task of explaining why his or her students should study history. Many reasons have been given. One is that lessons exist in the past from which contemporary society can benefit and learn. Another is that exploration of the past allows us to see the origins of our customs, ideas, and institutions. Concepts such as democracy, ethnic conflict, or even things as trivial as fashion or mores, have historical roots.

Reasons such as these impress few students, however. If anything, these explanations seem remote and dull to young minds. Yet history is anything but dull. And therein lies what is perhaps the most compelling reason for studying history: History is filled with great stories. The classic themes of literature and drama—love and sacrifice, hatred and revenge, injustice and betrayal, adversity and overcoming adversity—fill the pages of history books, feeding the imagination as well as any of the great works of fiction do.

The story of the Children's Crusade, for example, is one of the most tragic in history. In 1212 Crusader fever hit Europe. A call went out from the pope that all good Christians should journey to Jerusalem to drive out the hated Muslims and return the city to Christian control. Heeding the call, thousands of children made the journey. Parents bravely allowed many children to go, and entire communities were inspired by the faith of these small Crusaders. Unfortunately, many boarded ships were captained by slave traders, who enthusiastically sold the children into slavery as soon as they arrived at their destination. Thousands died from disease, exposure, and starvation on the long march across Europe to the Mediterranean Sea. Others perished at sea.

Another story, from a modern and more familiar place, offers a soul-wrenching view of personal humiliation but also the ability to rise above it. Hatsuye Egami was one of 110,000 Japanese Americans sent to internment camps during World War II. "Since yesterday we Japanese have ceased to be human beings," he wrote in his diary. "We are numbers. We are no longer Egamis, but the number 23324. A tag with that number is on every trunk, suitcase and bag. Tags, also, on our breasts." Despite such dehumanizing treatment, most internees worked hard to control their bitterness. They created workable communities inside the camps and demonstrated again and again their loyalty as Americans.

These are but two of the many stories from history that can be found in the pages of the Lucent Books World History series. All World History titles rely on sound research and verifiable evidence, and all give students a clear sense of time, place, and chronology through maps and timelines as well as text.

All titles include a wide range of authoritative perspectives that demonstrate the complexity of historical interpretation and sharpen the reader's critical thinking skills. Formally documented quotations and annotated bibliographies enable students to locate and evaluate sources, often instantaneously via the Internet, and serve as valuable tools for further research and debate.

Finally, Lucent's World History titles present rousing good stories, featuring vivid primary source quotations drawn from unique, sometimes obscure sources such as diaries, public records, and contemporary chronicles. In this way, the voices of participants and witnesses as well as important biographers and historians bring the study of history to life. As we are caught up in the lives of others, we are reminded that we too are characters in the ongoing human saga, and we are better prepared for our own roles.

Important Dates

1821
Mexican revolutionaries win self-rule from Spain; American law student Stephen Austin makes a deal with Mexican authorities to allow Americans to settle in Texas, then a Mexican province.

1794
Future Mexican president and Alamo besieger Antonio López de Santa Anna is born near Vera Cruz, Mexico.

1776
Britain's American colonies declare their independence, marking the birth of the United States.

1833
Santa Anna is elected president of Mexico and quickly becomes a tyrant.

1500	1775	1795	1815	1835

1500s
Spanish soldiers and settlers seize what is now Mexico from the local Native Americans.

1810
Priest Miguel Hidalgo leads the first popular Mexican rebellion against Spanish rule.

1835
Texian patriots under Austin besiege Santa Anna's brother-in-law, General Cos, in San Antonio; Cos eventually surrenders; the Texians declare Texas to be a Mexican state.

1786
Legendary frontiersman and future Alamo defender Davy Crockett is born in Tennessee.

1824
The Republic of Mexico is officially established.

1831
American military officer William Barret Travis leaves South Carolina and settles in Texas.

1829
Responding to American settlers' bringing slaves into Texas, Mexican leaders ban slavery within Mexico's borders.

of the Period

1845
Texas becomes the twenty-eighth U.S. state.

1955
An episode of renowned entertainer Walt Disney's popular TV program features a dramatization of Crockett's exploits at the Alamo; thereafter, an enormous Crockett craze sweeps the nation.

1892
The Daughters of the Republic of Texas, a group dedicated to preserving historic Texan monuments, is established and soon begins to raise money to refurbish and maintain the Alamo.

1911
The first movie about the Alamo, *The Immortal Alamo*, is made.

2004
Popular actor Billy Bob Thornton appears as Davy Crockett in the colorful, mostly historically accurate film *The Alamo*.

1840	1880	1920	1960	2000

1960
The Alamo becomes a U.S. National Historic Landmark; renowned actor John Wayne releases a spectacular film about the Alamo siege in which he portrays Crockett.

1975
A translation of the memoirs of Mexican officer José Enrique de la Peña is published; Peña's contention that some Alamo defenders, including Crockett, survived the battle and were later executed ignites much controversy.

1836
In February Santa Anna's army reaches San Antonio; Travis and Bowie order the Texian soldiers into the Alamo mission-fort; the siege of the Alamo begins. In March the Alamo falls to Santa Anna's army; all of the defenders are slain.

The Alamo in the Public Mind

In 1836, 187 men died while defending an old Spanish Catholic mission called the Alamo. Most of them were Americans. But a few had been born in other lands, including Mexico, England, Ireland, Scotland, Germany, and Denmark. The Alamo was then located on the outskirts of the small town of San Antonio de Bexar, in the Mexican federal district of Tejas, what is now southern Texas. Abandoned in the 1790s, the mission was subsequently used as a fort by soldiers of the Mexican army.

In 1835 a group of Texians attacked and expelled the Alamo's Mexican garrison. (At the time, residents of Texas were called Texians, as well as Texicans and Texonians. The term *Texan* developed later.) The following year Mexico's ambitious dictator, Antonio López de Santa Anna, led an army to San Antonio. At the end of a dramatic thirteen-day siege, he managed to capture the Alamo.

Thereafter, the fort's dead defenders, among them frontier legends Jim Bowie and Davy Crockett, were recognized as American heroes. The Alamo itself eventually became a symbol of courage and freedom to Texians and Americans alike. Some sections of the mission-fortress were preserved and today make up a shrine visited by thousands of people each year.

Sources of Alamo Images

The vast majority of those visitors find the experience inspiring. But many have difficulty envisioning what the Alamo looked like in 1836 and how the final battle transpired and felt. To a large degree this is because only a small portion of the original mission compound has survived. Also, the shrine is surrounded by offices, shops, and other buildings in the midst of a bustling modern city. So it is hard to picture it on an open plain, surrounded by thousands of Mexican troops, and suffering a days-long barrage of cannonballs.

To help the shrine's visitors, along with modern history buffs and school students in American history classes, a number of historians have penned accounts of that momentous event. Yet those written narratives are not what most people envision when they consider the Alamo's fall. Rather, the main images of the Alamo in the public mind come not from historians and other experts, but from filmmakers. As American scholars Randy Roberts and James S. Olson point out, somewhat to their regret, "More than 150 years after the storming of the Alamo, the two most important interpreters of the event are Walt Disney and John Wayne."[1]

Roberts and Olson here refer to two highly influential movie versions of the 1836 Alamo battle. The first was the February 1955 television rendition, *Davy Crockett at the Alamo*, presented by legendary entertainer Walt Disney on his original *Disneyland* program. (Later that year Disney released a feature film, *Davy Crockett: King of the Wild Frontier*, to movie theaters. In addition to *Davy Crockett at the Alamo*, it included other episodes from Crockett's life that had been shown on the TV show in 1954.)

The Alamo in San Antonio, Texas, has become a shrine for many Texans.

The second famous Alamo movie was the 1960 feature film *The Alamo*, produced and directed by widely popular actor John Wayne (who also played Crockett in the production). These were not the first movie versions of the Alamo siege, nor were they the last. At least eleven theatrical and television films depicting the main events of the battle have been made since 1911, along with numerous others dealing with individual characters and other aspects, both real and fictional.

A Davy Crockett Craze

However, Disney's and Wayne's versions were by far the most renowned, successful, and widely seen. Both men were highly patriotic and had always been fascinated by nineteenth-century American frontier heroes. Also, both had long dreamed of making a movie about those legendary figures.

For Disney, Davy Crockett was the main attraction. The real Crockett was a perfect subject for a family entertainment show appealing to both children

The Mexican army begins its assault on the Alamo in a scene from the 1960 film The Alamo. *No fewer than eleven theatrical versions of the events at the Alamo have been made since 1911.*

and their parents. A larger-than-life character, his homespun qualities, including a Tennessee drawl, buckskin coat, and coonskin cap, neatly complemented his adventures as a backwoods soldier, U.S. congressman, and martyr of the Alamo.

Disney told Crockett's life in three installments, broadcast in succeeding episodes of the *Disneyland* show. The title character was played by the then little-known actor Fess Parker, and his wise-cracking sidekick was portrayed by Buddy Ebsen, who later achieved stardom as Jed Clampett in the popular sitcom *The Beverly Hillbillies*.

Overall, the budget for Disney's Crockett miniseries was low. So in the third episode, about the Alamo's fall, the battle scenes were fairly small-scale and obviously filmed in a studio. Nevertheless, Parker and Ebsen were endearing in their roles, and Crockett's last moments in the climax of the battle were stirring. He is last seen swinging his rifle ("Ol Betsy") back and forth like a club at the dozens of Mexican soldiers who are converging on him. Although it is clear he will not survive, the camera moves away at the last moment, and the exact manner of the hero's demise is left to the viewer's imagination. This was fitting, for to this day historians and others continue to debate how Crockett died.

Disney's version of the Alamo siege was further ingrained in the public mind by the enormous Davy Crockett craze that swept America in the wake of the TV shows. On the one hand, there was an unprecedented merchandising bonanza. Children, or more accurately their parents, spent at least $100 million ($700 million in today's money) on Crockett coonskin caps, lunch boxes, comic books, food products, and much more. On the other hand, those same children became aware of the Alamo and its heroes for the first time, acted out its events, and cemented it permanently into their own mind's eye and the public's as well. As noted Crockett biographer Michael Wallis tells it, when he was a boy,

> the dusty hill topped by a stand of oaks on the edge of the playground became our Alamo, and every day we pretended that we were in pitched battle against the forces of Santa Anna. We became Davy Crockett, William Travis, and Jim Bowie, the trio of legendary Alamo heroes. No one wanted to be with the Mexican side, so our enemy . . . was largely invisible. In the end we died anyway, just as our heroes did so long ago, but we knew we would miraculously be resurrected and come back the next day for another round of combat.[2]

"To Die Decently"

Released six years after Disney's version, John Wayne's Alamo film even more powerfully burned the Alamo's epic story into the modern American consciousness. Wayne's preoccupation was less with Crockett and more with the heroics of the fort's defenders as a valiant fighting unit. Indeed, his goal was to remind his fellow Americans what Crockett, Travis, Bowie, and the rest had fought and died for. Namely, Wayne believed, it was a principle—the unique and highly desirable benefits of liberty that come from a democratic form of government, or a republic. At the time of the Alamo siege, the Texians were ruled by a Mexican dictator and wanted to break away and create a republic in which they could live and breathe free. So at one pivotal moment in the film, Wayne, as Crockett, summarized the republican concept well, saying:

> Republic. I like the sound of the word. It means people can live free, talk free, go or come, buy or sell, be drunk or sober, however they choose. Some words give you a feeling. Republic is one of those words that makes me tight in the throat—the same tightness a man gets when his baby takes his first step or his first baby shaves and makes his first sound as a man. Some words can give you a feeling that makes your heart warm. Republic is one of those words.[3]

Wayne further clarified this message in a press release for the movie. "I want to remind the freedom-loving people of the world," he said, "that not so long ago there were men and women in America who had the guts to stand up and fight for the things they believed in. . . . The people of the Alamo realized that in order to live decently a [person] must be prepared to die decently. There were no namby-pamby pussy-footers . . . in that brave band.[4]

An Epic Creation Myth

Thus, both Disney and Wayne had their own reasons for portraying the Alamo and its defenders the way they did. A few aspects of those film versions were presented fairly accurately. But most were not, and all true Alamo fans reach a point when, to their dismay, they discover that the real events did not always happen like they did on the silver screen. "Those of us who grew up with the Walt Disney version," noted Alamo scholar Stephen L. Hardin says, were upset to "hear that our childhood hero may not have gone down swinging Ol' Betsy *a la* Fess Parker."[5]

For a proper, accurate picture of what happened at the Alamo, then, one must turn to the accounts of trained historians. They are based primarily on eyewitness testimony in diaries, newspapers, written recollections, and other documents that survive from the nineteenth century. These sources do not tell the whole story. But they can be pieced together to create a surprisingly detailed and vivid portrait of what one expert calls "the epic creation myth of the Texas Republic and arguably the American West," a sweeping, action-packed, inspiring tale that "is still part of the American character today."[6]

Chapter One

Anglos Overrun the Texas Frontier

Today the vast majority of Americans above the age of twelve recognize the term *Alamo*. Many may not know precisely where that historic structure stands or the exact details of the battle for Texan freedom that transpired there. Yet, if only because so many movies have depicted it over the years, most people are aware that such a battle did take place. For that reason, as prolific American historian Edwin P. Hoyt points out, the simple mention of the Alamo quite often

> conjures visions of blood, sweat, and tears. Smells, sights, and sounds: the acrid stink of gunpowder, the gleaming steel of bayonets, the screams of frightened horses, the shouts of soldiers as they move to attack, the booming of cannon, and the popping of rifles and muskets. The cries of the wounded, and the awful silence of the dead. It was

not a big battle, [but after] it was over . . . [the battle cry] "Remember the Alamo!" [shook] the world.[7]

A Destiny to Expand?

There was a time, however, when the word *Alamo* was virtually unknown to every citizen of the United States. Indeed, this was the state of affairs roughly two centuries ago, between about 1810 and 1830, a period when the young country was rapidly and vigorously beginning to expand westward. Tens of thousands of settlers left the Eastern Seaboard and journeyed westward beyond the Appalachian Mountains in search of farmland, riches, and/or adventure. They cut down forests, planted crops, erected towns, and raised large families in what are now Kentucky, Tennessee, Ohio, Arkansas, and Alabama.

During that period a majority of Americans believed that this relentless growth and development was not only natural, but also morally right and even preordained by God. This idea emerged in the late 1700s and early 1800s. But it was not until the 1840s, a few years after the Alamo's fall, that a widely popular descriptive term for it materialized—Manifest Destiny. In short, this idea held that it was the ultimate fate of America to stretch across the continent from the Atlantic to the Pacific.

As early as 1801 the third U.S. president, Thomas Jefferson, had called attention to the seemingly limitless lands lying to the west. They would supply the nation with ample room for settlement for thousands of generations to come, he told his countrymen. At the time, however, he did not foresee that such expansion would be accomplished at the expense of other peoples who got in the settlers' way, notably the Indians and Mexicans. "Certainly," historian Irwin Unger remarks, "the peoples and nations who stood in the path of America's expansionist urge found it difficult to see it as divinely inspired and benevolent. And all too often, Manifest Destiny

An allegorical female figure representing Manifest Destiny leads American pioneers, telegraph wires, and railroads westward while native peoples and wildlife retreat before them. The theory of Manifest Destiny held that it was the ultimate fate of America to stretch across the continent.

A Land of "Savages and Wild Beasts"

Not all Americans of the early 1800s saw Manifest Destiny as inevitable, and some even felt it was neither wise nor good. One prominent example was Massachusetts statesman and orator Daniel Webster (1782–1852). "What do we want with this vast, worthless area?" he asked. "This region [is a land] of savages and wild beasts, of deserts, of shifting sands and whirlwinds of dust. . . . To what use could we ever hope to put these great deserts, or these endless mountain ranges? . . . I will never vote one cent from the public treasury to place the Pacific coast one inch nearer to Boston than it is now."

Quoted in John E. Weems. *To Conquer a Peace: The War Between the United States and Mexico*. College Station: Texas A&M University Press, 2000, p. 188.

would excuse the harshest disregard of the rights of others. It also reeked of cultural and racial arrogance that implied the superiority of American civilization . . . to any other in North America."[8]

"Gone to Texas"

Inspired by the notion that it was their God-given right to overrun and develop the western lands, American settlers inevitably came up against an enormous obstacle in their path. A large foreign nation, Mexico, had territories in these lands and stood squarely in the way of their dreams of Manifest Destiny. The first Mexican territory the westward stream of Americans encountered was the vast, sparsely inhabited Mexican frontier region called "Tejas" in Spanish and "Texas" in English. Some of the American settlers decided to go around Texas and continue their westward

trek well to the north of Mexican territory. But others saw little or no reason to avoid planting roots in the highly appealing area simply because it was owned by a foreign government.

So in the 1820s American homesteaders began moving into Texas. Large numbers of them were lured by ads placed in newspapers, guidebooks, and other written media painting inviting pictures of "smiling prairies" that were perfect for "the plow." All that a settler needed to succeed in Texas was a willingness to work hard, the ads promised. Further, "the reward of industry is so ample as to furnish the greatest incentive."[9]

These ads and other encouragements for Anglos, or white Americans, to settle in Texas were mostly supplied by *empresarios*. They were non-Mexicans to whom the Mexican government

Famed Mexican painter Diego Rivera did this portrait of Father José María Morelos, who led Mexican revolutionaries after the execution of his mentor, Father Hidalgo.

granted land holdings on Mexican soil in exchange for their recruitment of other foreign settlers. It was hoped that the settlers would develop some of the unused land and thereby increase its value. These efforts were very success- ful. As a result, people moving into the southeastern United States increasingly came upon abandoned farmhouses and trappers' cabins with the message "Gone to Texas" scrawled on the front doors.

Mexico's Fight for Independence

At first, Mexican officials paid only passing attention to this initial entry of Anglo settlers into Texas. One reason was that those leaders were preoccupied with a major struggle for independence from Spain. Mexico had long been a Spanish colony officially called New Spain. But by the early 1800s, many of the colony's residents had become discontented with Spanish rule and wanted to replace it with a democratic republic headed by leaders elected by the people.

The people of Mexico were encouraged partly by the successful American Revolution that had created the United States only a few decades before. Another major inspiration was the French Revolution of 1789. Like the American one, it had been driven by people's fervent desire to govern themselves.

The first of several Mexican rebellions against Spain took place in 1810. A priest named Miguel Hidalgo became leader of a large group of peasants, priests, and others who sought the removal of Spanish officials, whom they accused of injustice and brutality against middle-class and especially lower-class Mexicans. The fearful officials soon unleashed a small army of trained soldiers on the protesters, who were easily crushed. Hidalgo was captured and executed.

Thereafter, however, Hidalgo was widely seen as a martyr and popular folk hero, and the cause of Mexican independence gained steam. In 1813 and 1814 Hidalgo's close follower José María Morelos took charge of a better-organized insurrection. The rebels managed to seize control of most of southern Mexico, but they, too, were eventually defeated by government forces. It was not until 1821 that a revolutionary movement succeeded in Mexico. This time thousands of clergy and well-to-do landowners joined the rebels, and in August 1821 they forced the Spanish to grant Mexico its independence.

Once the nation was free of the Spanish government, Mexico's leaders did not agree on who should rule and how. Serious disagreements and infighting occurred in the three years that followed, and only in 1824 was the new national legislature able to officially establish the Republic of Mexico. It adopted a constitution similar in some, but certainly not all, ways to that of the United States.

Enter the Austins

Mexican leaders also divided the country into nineteen states and four territories. Texas was the northern section of a state called Coahuila y Tejas. Overall, these lands were vast and largely undeveloped. In addition to the geographical expanse Mexico now covers, in those days it encompassed what are now Texas, New Mexico, Arizona, and parts of Colorado, Nevada, and California. That made a total of about 1,901,600 square miles (4,925,121 sq. km), equivalent to just over half the present size of the United States.

Mexico's new leaders hoped to populate some of these enormous vacant lands with hardworking new citizens imported from other nations. (It is important to emphasize that the lands were "vacant" only in the eyes of Mexican and U.S. officials. Thousands of Native Americans dwelled in various sectors of Mexican territory. But the Mexicans and Americans did not view the Indians as the owners of those lands and regularly disregarded their rights

Stephen F. Austin negotiated settlement deals with the Mexican government and settled hundreds of American families in southern Texas.

and at times their very existence.) Mexico's leaders hoped the incoming settlers would create farms, towns, and roads, thereby making the country stronger and richer. To that end, between 1824 and 1825 the government instituted successive laws promoting such immigration, including the entry of Anglos into Texas.

Some Mexican officials in this period worried that the passage of these laws and the resulting influx of American settlers might create social and other problems for Mexico. But they were initially overruled by those who insisted that the new nation should work hard to develop its thinly populated provinces. The pro-immigration officials tended to believe the rosy pictures painted by *empresarios* like Americans Moses and Stephen Austin. Moses Austin was a frontier entrepreneur (enterprising businessman) and colonizer. Back in January 1821, during the revolutionary period, he had persuaded a high-ranking Mexican official to set aside 200,000 acres (80,937ha) of Texas land for settlement by Anglos.

However, when Austin unexpectedly died just six months later, it appeared the deal was null and void. At that point his son, Stephen, who was then at law school in New Orleans, stepped in and told the Mexicans he would carry on his father's work. The younger Austin proposed that each family head be allowed to buy 640 acres (259ha), along with 320 acres (129.5ha) for his wife and 160 acres (64.75ha) for each of his children, for the low price of 12.5 cents per acre.

When the Mexicans agreed to this arrangement, Austin advertised for colonists and swiftly settled hundreds of them in fertile farming areas along the Brazos and Colorado Rivers in southern Texas. The only catch was that at first the Mexican government would not commit to maintaining garrisons of soldiers in the faraway province. To protect the new communities from Indians and pirates, Austin was obliged to raise a small militia from among the settlers themselves.

The Promised Land

During the thirteen years that followed, Stephen Austin successfully negotiated several more land agreements with the Mexican government. By 1824 some four thousand Anglos had made new homes in Texas, and by 1830 the number had risen to sixteen thousand. These early settlers were well aware that nearly all of the lands they were entering were undeveloped and that mere survival would require concentrated and backbreaking work. Indeed, as scholars Tim J. Todish and Terry S. Todish write,

Life on the Texas frontier demanded constant work from almost everyone. For field animals and homemakers, this was tremendously taxing. But for those "bringing home the bacon" [that is, the male heads of families], there was a unique benefit. Much of the diet was filled by game, and hunting was a frequent occupation. This led

one woman to observe that Texas was "Hell for women and oxen, [but] Heaven for men and dogs."[10]

In addition, the frontier held a number of dangers for the white settlers, the most problematic of which was raiding by local Indian tribes. Many of the Native Americans viewed the whites as interlopers who did not belong there, and this sometimes led to violence. A surviving eyewitness account by an early Tejano (teh-HAHN-oh, a Mexican-born settler) who resided in San Antonio shows how dangerous the town was in the 1820s: "Although the land is most fertile, the inhabitants do not cultivate it because of the danger of Indians which they face as soon as they separate themselves any distance from their houses, to which these barbarians come often in the silence of the night to do damage without fear of [anyone stopping them]."[11]

The newly arriving Anglo settlers in the region responded to the perceived threats posed by Indians and pirates by creating small groups of mounted guards. The forerunners of the Texas Rangers, they patrolled the prairies to try to keep those threats at bay. Yet in spite of such dangers, along with the seemingly endless and exhausting work required to make a living, the new settlers rarely complained. Most of these pioneers, Todish and Todish point out, "felt they had found the Promised Land,"[12] much like the one the wandering Hebrews had populated in the Bible.

Texas's "Potent Magnets"

In the late 1820s and early 1830s, increasing numbers of Americans became part of the "gone to Texas" crowd, each person or family having his or its own "magnets," or reasons for going, as noted by the late expert on Texas history Nathaniel Stephenson.

From every section [of the country], from every class, pilgrims were drawn to Texas, the very seat of fortune in the American mind during the [1820s]. Its noble woods, its great prairies, the land that could be had for next to nothing—these were potent magnets. Furthermore, it was the land of romance, of mystery. It was the borderland of the strange Spanish world. To the adventurous soul, it called in the deep murmur of the forest, in the wind across the trackless prairie—"I am the Unknown!" To the dreamer of democracy, it whispered grimly of possible revolution, of the last death-struggle between the people and the kings. The upholder of slavery saw in Texas a possible new lease of life for his peculiar institution. The abolitionist saw in it the possibility of new free state. . . . Young and old, rich and poor, wise and foolish, a great host of Americans poured into the colonies of Texas in the high days of the [1820s].

Nathaniel Stephenson. *Texas and the Mexican War*. Charleston, SC: Nabu, 2010, pp. 10–11.

During the late 1820s and early 1830s increasing numbers of Americans caught "Gone to Texas" fever. Wide-open spaces and cheap land were the big draw.

Serious Breaches of Promise

Austin knew that the American frontier families were industrious and would do what was necessary to tame the land. So he confidently told Mexican leaders that the growing Anglo settlements would boost the value of that land. They would also produce considerable tax revenues that would swell Mexico's national treasury, he predicted.

However, the rest of Austin's forecasts about the behavior of the colonists he had recruited later proved considerably less accurate. For example, he claimed that in addition to paying Mexican taxes, the settlers would convert to Catholicism, Mexico's predominant faith. Austin also promised that the Anglos who entered Texas would obey Mexico's laws and become good Mexican citizens. He laid down rules for such ethical and patriotic behavior in the general regulations he formulated for the colony. "No person will be admitted as a settler, who does not produce satisfactory evidence of having supported the character of a moral, sober, and industrious citizen," the first rule stated. The second said, "Each settler must, when called on by the Governor of said Province, take the oath of allegiance to the government exercising the sovereignty of the country."[13]

The settlers promised to uphold these rules, but while a few did obey them, many did not. To Austin's and Mexican officials' disdain, increasing numbers of the immigrants broke their word. Numerous Texians, as the residents of Texas came to call themselves, refused to maintain allegiance to a government they viewed as culturally and politically alien. They also balked at paying certain trade tariffs imposed by the government, as did some local Tejanos who had come to befriend and agree with their Anglo neighbors. Many Texians felt that the government was faraway, faceless, and remote from their lives. Moreover, it had given them no real say in how they were governed. So why should they pay government-imposed tariffs that did not directly benefit them?

Moreover, most of the American-born Texians refused to become Catholics. They had grown up in a country that guaranteed freedom of religion, and it did not seem right to them that they should be forced to follow a specific faith. In comparison, Mexican officials saw the refusal to adopt Catholicism as a serious breach of promise. There was no freedom of religion in Mexico, and all Mexican citizens were expected to follow the Catholic Church's teachings. Becoming Catholic, the government argued, was part of the deal the settlers had agreed to in exchange for their plots of land. So they should honor the agreement.

No less grave an offense in Mexican eyes was the issue of the Anglo immigrants bringing their black slaves with them into Mexican territory. The first twenty thousand Americans who settled in Texas were accompanied by at least two thousand slaves. This caused friction and resentment between the settlers and the government in Mexico City because as time went on, most Mexicans came to disapprove of slavery. This was

"The Richest Country in the World"

The tremendous appeal of large portions of Texas to Americans in the early nineteenth century was ably captured by famous frontiersman Davy Crockett, who ended up dying for the cause of Texas's independence. These words come from a letter he wrote to his son and daughter on January 9, 1836, fewer than two months before his death at the Alamo.

I must say, as to what I have seen of Texas, it is the garden spot of the world. The best land and the best prospect for health I ever saw is here, and I do believe it is a fortune to any man to come here. There is a world of country to settle. . . . I expect in all probability to settle on the Bodark or Choctaw Bayou of [the] Red River. That, I have no doubt, is the richest country in the world. [It has] good land and plenty of timber, and the best springs and good mill streams. [There are also] good range[s], clear water, and ever [an] appearance of good health, and [of] game [there's] plenty. It is in the pass where the buffalo passes from the north to south and back twice a year, and [of] bees and honey [there are] plenty.

Quoted in Texian Legacy Association. "David Crockett's Letter to His Children." www.texianlegacy.com /crockettletter.html.

reflected to some degree in the 1824 Constitution, which condemned slavery, and much more strongly in an 1829 decree that freed all slaves in Mexico. In response, the settlers who owned slaves argued that slavery was part of their way of life and integral to their ability to make a living. It was not fair, they said, for the government to strip them of their long-held right to own slaves.

Hearing this argument, Mexican legislators reluctantly decided to make an exception. To accommodate the Anglo slaveholders, the government created a legal exemption that allowed them to keep their existing slaves. But further importation of slaves was banned, and all children born of slaves in Mexico were to be free. Not surprisingly, the Texian slave owners were outraged. A number of them ignored the new laws, and a few started pushing for independence from Mexico so they could have as many slaves as they wanted. Thus, as Randy Roberts and James S. Olson point out, "the American heroes who would die at the Alamo were fighting for many causes—including slavery."[14]

A Wedge of Distrust

Eventually, the continuing influx of Anglos into Texas and the flouting of Mexican laws by those newcomers became too much for a majority of Mexican leaders. The national legislature reacted by passing new immigration laws that limited the number of Americans who could settle in Texas. Mexican leaders were surprised when most of the Texians ignored these laws as well.

This unfortunate situation increasingly drove a wedge of distrust between members of the two cultures. The settlers came to view the Mexican government as overbearing, repressive, and opposed to individual freedom and civil rights. Their overall attitude was reflected in a document penned by a small group of Texians in the town of Anahuac, near Galveston, in June 1832. Feeling repressed by the local Mexican garrison, they staged a minor insurrection and issued a list of resolutions to justify their actions. They chastised the government for its "repeated violations of the constitution, laws, and [its] total disregard of the civil and political rights of the people." Furthermore, they stated, "we view with feelings of the deepest regret the manner in which the Government of the Republic of Mexico [has perpetrated] a military despotism . . . of such character as to arouse the feelings of every freeman and impel him to resistance."[15]

In sharp contrast, meanwhile, not only officials in Mexico City but also many

This Catholic mission near San Antonio was built by the Spanish in 1731. Tensions rose between American settlers and the Mexican government over the requirement that all settlers convert to Catholicism.

YOUNG TEXAS IN REPOSE.

A political cartoon depicts a grotesque Texan sitting on a slave. Although the Mexican government outlawed slavery, it created a legal exemption that allowed Americans to keep their slaves.

ordinary Mexicans increasingly came to see Americans as ill-mannered, vulgar, and unlawful ingrates. One extremely disappointed and irritated Mexican official stated that the government should "take measures to prevent the planting of a population [in Texas] composed of abominable people of bad conduct."[16] In the same vein, a circular distributed by the Mexican government's minister of relations noted:

The colonists established in Texas have recently given the most unequivocal evidence of the extrem-ity to which [deception], ingratitude, and the restless spirit that animates them can go, since forgetting what they owe to the supreme government of the nation which so generously admitted them to its bosom, gave them fertile lands to cultivate, and allowed them all the means to live in comfort and abundance—they have risen against that same government . . . [while] concealing their criminal purpose of dismembering the territory of the Republic.[17]

Mexico's minister to the United States, Manuel Eduardo de Gorostiza, agreed fully with the ugly portrait of Americans painted by these words. A highly educated and cultured person, he claimed he had frequently been treated with disrespect by American diplomats. This caused him to become scornful of many Americans, and he said of the Anglo settlers:

Let us consider the character of those who have populated the lands adjoining our border. Who is not familiar with that race of migratory adventurers that exist in the United States, composed of the most reckless, profligate [wasteful], and robust of its sons, who always live in the unpopulated regions? . . . Far removed from civilization, as they condescendingly call it, they are precursors of immorality and pillage. . . . [They] take possession of a new land and remain there for one or two years, building a log cabin for shelter, and when they grow tired of the place they sell it to others, less daring than they. Then once more, with hatchet in hand and rifle on shoulder, they go in search of new lands.[18]

Those "new lands" might well eventually grow into *all* of Texas, still another government leader warned. "Mexicans!" he thundered in a session of the national legislature. "Watch closely, for you know only too well the [Anglos'] greed for territory! . . . They may conspire with the United States to take Texas from us. From this time [on], be on your guard!"[19] In time, this ominous prophecy would come to pass. But before it could, much blood—Texian and Mexican alike—would be spilled in Texas.

Chapter Two

Bloodshed Sparks Open Rebellion

By 1834 more than thirty thousand Anglos from the nearby American states had settled down in Texas. The Tejanos in the region—most of them farmers and cattle ranchers of modest means—numbered roughly seventy-five hundred. Although some of the Tejanos sympathized with the revolutionary, antigovernment view, most did not. So the Anglos and native Mexicans in Texas often found themselves at odds politically and otherwise. Many Tejanos resented the former Americans for bringing slaves into the area, for purposely ignoring Mexican laws, and for refusing to convert to Catholicism.

Growing numbers of Anglo Texians had come to resist the government in one way or another, and some even leaned toward the idea of Texian independence. Also by this time, some Anglos openly admitted that they had taken the oath of allegiance to Mexico only to get their hands on fertile farm- or grazing lands.

They had never intended to become loyal Mexican citizens, and the recent repressive actions of the government had only reinforced that stance.

Meanwhile, Mexican officials in the faraway capital had become thoroughly aggravated by a group of what they saw as irritating troublemakers in Texas. The problem was what to do about them. Mexican legislators had passed laws restricting or punishing the settlers in one way or another. But for the most part, these moves had proved ineffective and futile. This was due partly to the government's own instability. Power changed hands often during the 1820s as leaders came and went, and most of them had been more interested in preserving their own authority than facing and fixing problems in the distant provinces.

The very fact of that distance was another problem. Almost 800 miles (1,287km) of rugged wilderness with few roads and towns separated Mexico City from the Texas settlements. That made marching a large army to those towns an extremely time-consuming and expensive undertaking.

Nevertheless, as tensions continued to rise between the settlers and the government, isolated violent episodes increased in number. These steadily escalated into small battles in which both sides suffered casualties. What had been mainly revolutionary talk soon grew into open rebellion, and the government came to realize that it had to respond with overwhelming force or else lose Texas forever.

War Inevitable?

People on both sides of this conflict came to feel that violence over the Texas situation was inevitable. All-out war may well have been avoidable. But that would have necessitated restraint and compromise by the opposing leaders, and by 1834–1835 those in charge on each side felt that the "enemy" had already pushed them too far.

This inflexible attitude was expressed on the Mexican side by the words of nineteenth-century Mexican journalist, statesman, and historian Carlos María de Bustamente. Speaking for most of his fellow citizens, he stated that the rebellious Texians were not patriots fighting for liberty, as they claimed to be. Rather, they were nothing but slippery swindlers who had made a deal and then welched on it.

Mexico was not at fault, Bustamente insisted, for it had not asked the settlers for any sort of payment in exchange for Mexican land. Also, it had bestowed on them various special liberties, including "ten years' exemption in the payment" of taxes and permission "to sell their products to the other Mexican states." Moreover, he said,

the colonists accepted these terms and—mark this well—placed no conditions upon them. Rather, they promised to be faithful to the Mexican Republic of which they now formed a part. . . . [Mexico] inflicted upon Texas [no] wrongs of any kind—unless one qualifies as wrongs the giving of lands without receiving any compensation. Mexico, therefore, took the view that its generosity was repaid by an act of ingratitude, and it could do no less than to consider some of the inhabitants of Texas . . . to be colonists in rebellion who, for the honor and dignity of the government, must be repressed by force.[20]

On the Texian side, in comparison, the push toward violence and war was based in large part on the right to freedom from tyrannical government. An increasingly bigger percentage of the settlers felt they were entitled to that right because they had grown up in the United States. The late scholar Amelia W. Williams explains how this attitude led to the formation of hardened factions within the Texian community. The troubled situation in Texas in the early 1830s, she said, kept ever prominent the question: "What is to be the future of Texas? Shall it remain a province of Mexico? . . . Shall it seek to become an independent nation? Or shall it ask for annexation to the United States? . . . [The more] intelligent Mexican officials of Texas honestly believed that there was a strong sentiment throughout the American settlements for separation from Mexico. [Indeed] there was a good deal of loose talk on the part of hot-headed persons on both sides of the American boundary line. . . . [Over time] two strong parties developed among the Texians. . . . One, the peace party, was composed of the conservatives. They were the calm-minded men who believed, with Austin, in "ironing out" their differences and in conciliating the Mexican officials, thereby remaining loyal to their adopted country. The other, the war party . . . wanted to fight for what they regarded as their rights.[21]

"Texas Is Lost"

Manuel de Mier y Terán was one of Mexico's best and most responsible generals during the Texas Revolution. Unlike Santa Anna and most of the other Mexican leaders, he was a staunch realist and recognized early on that Mexico's loss of Texas to the Anglo settlers was inevitable. On July 2, 1832, the day before his death by suicide, he dejectedly wrote to a friend:

A great and respectable Mexican nation, a nation of which we have dreamed and for which we have labored so long, can never emerge from the many disasters which have overtaken it. We have allowed ourselves to be deceived by the ambitions of selfish groups; and now we are about to lose the northern provinces. How could we expect to hold Texas when we do not even agree among ourselves? It is a gloomy state of affairs. If we could work together, we would advance. As it is, we are lost. . . . My soul is burdened with weariness. I am an unhappy man, and unhappy people should not live on earth. I have studied this situation for five years and today, I know nothing, nothing, for man is very despicable and small; and let us put an end to these reflections, for they almost drive me mad. The revolution is about to break forth and Texas is lost.

Quoted in Wallace L. McKeehan, ed. "Manuel de Mier y Terán, 1789–1832." Sons of Dewitt Colony Texas. www.tamu.edu/faculty/ccbn/dewitt/teranmanuel.htm#anarchy.

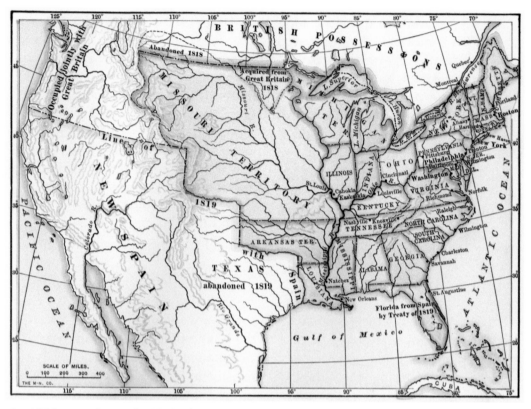

An 1819 map shows the United States and New Spain (Mexico), of which Texas was still a part.

"Come and Take It"

Stripped to the basics, therefore, the Texas Revolution of the mid-1830s was primarily a conflict between one group that felt its rights were being restricted and another that felt it had been forced to restrict those rights.

One of those restrictions turned out to be the proverbial last straw for a number of Texians. It took the form of an 1835 governmental decree designed to disarm the provincial militias. The person in charge in Mexico City at the time—General Santa Anna—had plans to turn Mexico into a dictatorship. If his own soldiers were the only ones with guns,

his thinking went, he would encounter no credible resistance to his authority.

But in issuing the controversial decree, Santa Anna did not anticipate the outrage that would arise among the vast majority of Anglo Texians. Virtually all of them owned guns for hunting, protection against Indians, or other reasons. Moreover, as former Americans they were used to living under the Second Amendment of the U.S. Constitution, which guarantees the right of citizens to bear arms. Trying to disarm such individuals would be the equivalent of stirring up a nest of angry hornets.

This became clear on October 2, 1835, when a band of Mexican troops tried to seize a small brass cannon from the residents of the town of Gonzales, not far east of San Antonio. On receiving an order from a Mexican officer to turn over the weapon, some of the defiant locals pieced together and displayed a flag bearing an image of the cannon and beneath it the words "Come and Take It." One of the Gonzales defenders, Creed Taylor, later recalled what happened when the Mexican soldiers took that dare and attempted to confiscate the cannon.

> During the night, the Mexicans had fallen back a short distance and taken position on a mound. While reconnoitering [observing], our scouts were fired upon, and as they fell back upon our line the Mexicans, about twenty-five or thirty in number, charged toward our position. [We fired the cannon and the shock] seemed to jar the very earth and the sound seemed sufficient to awaken the dead. It awoke the echoes for miles around and, figuratively, it continues to reverberate around the earth as the gun that sounded the death knell of Mexican tyranny in Texas. At the discharge of the cannon the Mexicans wheeled and fled with all speed to their main line, while their flight was greeted with a round of cheers such as only exultant [jubilant] Texans could give.[22]

Santa Anna's Rise to Power

On hearing about the resistance in Gonzales, Santa Anna was naturally frustrated, as he now realized it would be more difficult than he had thought to bring Texas under his control. It was his order to disarm the local settlers that in a very real sense set the Texas Revolution in motion and led to the Battle of the Alamo. So it is essential to consider how he rose to power and found himself in direct opposition to the Texians he would end up besieging in that now iconic fort.

In fairness to Antonio López de Santa Anna, he did not start out as the corrupt, cardboard villain so often depicted in the Alamo films. He grew up near Vera Cruz and in 1810, at the age of twelve, he lied about his age and enlisted as a cadet in the Spanish army. Over the ensuing years, he proved himself an effective soldier and showed much potential as a leader. Cited for bravery, he rose steadily through the ranks, along the way switching to the side of native Mexicans who were fighting for independence from Spain. Eventually, he became a general for reasons well deserved.

In that capacity, Santa Anna acted as a military adviser to Augustin de Iturbide, who early in 1822 declared himself emperor of the recently independent nation of Mexico. However, Iturbide was unpopular both with members of Congress and with most military officers. So in February 1823, seeing an opportunity to enhance his own image, Santa Anna marched an army on Mexico City and forced Iturbide to abdicate his throne.

After helping draft the 1824 Constitution, Santa Anna announced that he was retiring to private life. Yet for several years he exercised much power behind the scenes until finally becoming president of Mexico in April 1833. Up until that time his public image had remained largely positive. He had been widely admired by most Mexicans and a majority of Texians, too, as a strong advocate of republican values and democratic government.

A Desire for Glory

But not long after assuming the presidency, Santa Anna dissolved Congress and began fashioning a dictatorship supported by the army. He had long possessed an arrogant streak, which grew stronger over time. Added to this, it appears that as he grew older, he became increasingly infatuated with himself and with wielding power over others. One high-placed Mexican of that era said of him, "He gets carried away by an irresistible desire to

Augustin de Iturbide enters Mexico City in 1822 and declares himself emperor of Mexico. Antonio López de Santa Anna, however, led an army into Mexico City and forced Iturbide to abdicate.

Santa Anna a Paradox

Both American and Mexican historians agree that Santa Anna was a divisive and at times eccentric leader. Depending on the situation, people either loved or hated him, and similarly either laughed at or feared him. Underprivileged and illiterate Mexicans frequently viewed him as a dedicated champion of the people working hard to improve the country. But more educated and astute Mexicans recognized his personal ambition, arrogance, and mean streak. This notion—that he was a paradox who possessed a strange mixture of positive and negative attributes—was well articulated by a Mexican statesman and scholar of that era, Lucas Alamán. He said that Santa Anna had many talents but lacked a sturdy moral center. Also, the dictator had "an enterprising spirit, but [was] lacking in fixed purpose or determined objectives. [Further, his] energy and [strong] disposition for governing [were] obscured by great [ethical] defects, [while he showed a] clarity of perception in forming general plans for a revolution or campaign, yet great ineptitude in the directing of a battle."

Quoted in Cecil Robinson, ed. and trans. *The View from Chapultepec: Mexican Writers on the Mexican-American War*. Tucson: University of Arizona Press, 1989, p. xiv.

General Antonio Lopez de Santa Anna was a competent military commander but also a vainglorious man bent on dictatorship.

acquire glory," and defeat "maddens him."[23]

It became abundantly clear that the dictator had not only come to view himself as better than his fellow citizens, but also seemed to believe he was somehow heaven-sent to take control of Mexico. Historian Jeff Long quips, "He did not have a messiah complex. He skipped that level. He thought he *was* God."[24] Another modern expert adds that in his public life, Santa Anna was frequently irresponsible, and "his private life became vulgar and corrupt." He collected and wore "fantastic uniforms," was guilty of much "callous cruelty," cavorted with "hordes of passing whores," and was both infatuated with all things "superficial" and "a disastrous ruler."[25]

The dictator's obnoxious personal attributes aside, by mid-1835 only the state militias, a few of which were large and strong, blocked his way to ultimate power. That is why he gave the order to disarm them. Fortunately for him, there turned out to be little resistance from most of these militias. But it became clear that two states would be more problematic—Zacatecas, in north-central Mexico, and Texas, lying even farther north.

Indeed, most of the inhabitants of Zacatecas refused to accept Santa Anna as the country's leader, and local officials called out their militia to protect the state from him. Apparently, they assumed that this brave stand would intimidate him. But this proved to be a grave miscalculation. Still as fearless as ever, he promptly gathered thousands of federal troops, marched north, and invaded Zacatecas. Having defeated the local militia, he let loose his soldiers, who in a disgraceful three-day-long rampage looted, raped, and murdered the citizenry. One historian elaborates:

In the city alone [Santa Anna] captured twenty-four hundred prisoners and over a hundred officers. [He] decreed that all foreigners with the Zacatecan army be shot on the spot, but his own officers protested so loudly that he rescinded the order and allowed them to be marched in shackles to Mexico City. No one has finally determined the number of rebels killed in the battle or executed as prisoners, but Mexican historians continue to treat the brutal suppression of Zacatecans as a dark, shameful episode. Estimates of rebels and civilians killed in the ensuing rape and massacre range from the hundreds to twenty-five hundred. Plunder was the order of the day, and a special hatred was shown toward the few English and U.S. citizens in town. Their property was destroyed, some of the men were killed, and the women were treated shamefully.[26]

The Army of the People

Victorious over the Zacatecan rebels, Santa Anna, who by this time saw himself as invincible, turned his attention to Texas. Like the insolent Zacatecans, he reasoned, the Anglo Texians were disobedient rabble-rousers who must be reined in. To achieve that goal, in the early autumn of 1835 he sent his brother-in-law, General Martín Perfecto de Cos, to Texas.

Cos set out by sea from Vera Cruz with a small contingent of troops and landed at Copano Bay, bordering Rockport, Texas, on September 21, 1835. He then marched his men northwestward toward San Antonio, about 135 miles (217km) distant. Cos conceitedly assumed he had the upper hand and that the settlers would be overawed by him and his soldiers. Stating his position, he made it clear that he was there because the Texians were going against the Mexican Constitution, the very document they claimed Santa Anna was violating by demanding they disarm. "The plans of the revolutionists in Texas are well known," he said. "It is quite useless and vain to cover them with hypocritical adherence to the federal constitution. The constitution by which all Mexicans may be governed is the constitution which the colonists of Texas *must* obey, no matter on what *principles* it may be formed."[27]

Cos soon reached San Antonio and took charge of the roughly fourteen hundred Mexican soldiers then stationed there. His presence and purpose in Texas was not lost on the rebellious Texians. Their tempers flaring, a group of them rose up against a smaller Mexican garrison in the town of Goliad, lying about 30 miles (48km) north of Copano Bay. The Texians drove the Mexican garrison out of Goliad. Then they met in Gonzales and elected Stephen Austin as the provisional commander of what they called the "Army of the People." The all-volunteer force consisted of about three hundred men, a motley array dressed in all sorts of colorful western outfits and armed with flintlock rifles, shotguns, and knives.

San Antonio Besieged

Austin sent around ninety of these fighters under Jim Bowie and James Fannin to scout out a useful base of operations from which to oppose Cos's forces. Bowie and Fannin found what looked like a properly defensible position about 2 miles (3.2km) from San Antonio. The Texians weighed their choices. They could attack the town directly, which would involve a lot of one-on-one fighting and result in a fair amount of bloodshed. Or they could lay siege to it by surrounding the city and trapping the Mexican army inside without access to food or supplies until that army surrendered. They chose the latter course, hoping it might prevent bloodshed on both sides.

The siege began on October 27, 1835. The eminently civilized and considerate Austin did not want the Mexican soldiers actually to starve if it could be avoided. So early on he called on Cos to recognize the hopelessness of the Mexican situation and give up. In a November 1 letter to Bowie and Fannin, who were meeting with leading rebels elsewhere, Austin said:

I sent in a demand today for a surrender [to] Gen. Cos . . . [but] it was returned unopened. He in a short time after sent out Padre Garza [a local priest] with a [white] flag [of truce] to say to me, verbally, that he had absolute orders from his government to fortify [San Antonio de] Bexar and hold it at all hazards, and that as a military man his honor and duty required obedience to these orders, and that he would defend the place until he died, if he had only ten men left with him.[28]

As time went on, however, the Mexicans faced gradually worsening conditions that made Cos's stance increasingly less rigid. In particular, his men were unable to leave San Antonio to forage for food, so they steadily used up their army rations as well as existing supplies in the town. By December 4 the besiegers felt the enemy had been weakened enough and that the time was right for a large-scale assault, which began the next morning. A member of the Texian forces, Joseph Lopez, later described it, saying in part:

The firing commenced in earnest. . . . Flame and lead poured out [of our guns] as fast as the men could load and fire. Thus things went on for a few hours, when the officers set some of the men to digging trenches for the purpose of taking possession of other houses. . . . On the second day a large gun [cannon] was placed in the rear of [a] house, which being pointed towards the church steeple, made that portion of the edifice

tremble, in spite of its being built of stone, and dislodged those rascals [snipers, who] from that place [had been] picking [out] our men one at a time with their muskets. . . . It was [on] the fourth day that [a] night attack was planned for the taking of

Jim Bowie (pictured), along with James Fannin, led a siege of San Antonio in 1835, forcing the Mexican army there to surrender.

the plaza [town square], where the Mexicans were in strength. [When our men] opened their fire . . . [it] produced such a panic that . . . more than a hundred [Mexicans] were [accidentally] shot by their own companions, [and] this brought a flag of truce to us.[29]

An Army of Vengeance

The man who approached the Texians to ask for the truce was one of Cos's officers, Colonel José Juan Sánchez Navarro. The latter was shocked at the small number and scruffy appearance of the men who had defeated close to two thousand well-trained Mexican soldiers. He later recalled, "We were surrounded by crude bumpkins, proud and overbearing."[30]

General Cos soon signed a formal surrender document, officially ending the siege. In the weeks that followed, he undoubtedly dreaded having to face the dictator who had sent him to rein in the rebels. But to his surprise and relief, Santa Anna did not let loose his fury on

General Cos's Surrender Terms

When General Martín Perfecto de Cos surrendered to the Texians at the end of the siege of San Antonio in December 1835, he agreed to a number of stipulations, or conditions, some of which are listed here.

That general Cos and his officers [must] retire into the interior of [Mexico], under parole of honor; [and] that they will not in any way oppose the re-establishment of the federal Constitution of 1824. . . . That all the public property, money, arms and munitions of war be inventoried and delivered to [the Texian commander] General Burleson. That all private property [taken by the Mexicans in San Antonio] be restored to its proper owners. That three officers of each army be appointed to make out the inventory, and see that the terms of the capitulation [surrender] be carried into effect. . . . That general Cos with his force, for the present, occupy the Alamo; and General Burleson, with his force, occupy the town of [San Antonio]; and that the soldiers of neither party pass [by] the other armed. [That] General Cos shall, within six days from the date hereof, remove his force from the garrison he now occupies.

Texas State Library and Archives Commission. "Surrender Terms Signed by General Cos and General Burleson at San Antonio, December 11, 1835." www.tsl.state.tx.us/treasures/republic/bexar/cos1.html.

his ashamed brother-in-law. Indeed, the fact that they were family may have been the reason that Cos was not demoted or otherwise punished for his defeat.

Santa Anna instead directed his anger at the Texians, who in his estimation were in open, armed rebellion and needed to be taught a hard lesson. "I shall send four to six thousand men to Texas," he announced, "with the purpose of punishing those turbulent, insolent North Americans." Not long afterward, while amassing that fearsome army of vengeance, he vowed, "If they resist in the least . . . I shall convert Texas into a desert."[31]

Chapter Three

Santa Anna's Army Invades Texas

I f nothing else, Santa Anna was a man of his word. Fulfilling his promise to move against the rebellious Texians, in late December 1835 he swiftly began assembling large units of soldiers under his most trusted generals. One large brigade, commanded by General Joaquín Ramírez y Sesma and containing about 1,540 men, was already stationed at Rio Grande. A town lying just south of the major river of the same name, it was only a few days' march from San Antonio. The plan was for these soldiers to join up with the army's main body in the near future.

The units of that main body came together farther south, at San Luis Potosí, about 365 miles (587km) from San Antonio. To General Antonio Gaona, Santa Anna assigned some 1,600 troops, and General Eugenio Tolsa took charge of about 1,840 infantry (foot soldiers). Counting Sesma's troops and a couple of additional smaller cavalry units, the total army numbered just over 6,000 men.

Many of these soldiers had recently seen action in the bloody Zacatecan campaign. But Santa Anna felt this was not enough military schooling. Still in several ways an effective soldier, he drilled them, along with a number of greener recruits, in standard battle tactics for more than two weeks in Saltillo, lying several miles north of San Luis Potosí. On January 25, 1836, the dictator-general inspected the troops, clad in their neatly pressed green-and-white uniforms, in a grand review. Then, to the sound of flutes and drums, he marched them northward. On February 12 they linked up with Sesma's brigade, as planned, at Rio Grande. Soon afterward the army headed into the Texas frontier toward what Santa Anna expected would be a victorious date with destiny.

State of the Texian Military

Meanwhile, word that Santa Anna was gathering an army spread through southern Texas. This caused considerable anxiety among the settlers, as they knew that no centralized, official state army then existed in Texas to counter Santa Anna's hordes. Instead, the Texian resistance forces were divided among numerous small, informal units of militia.

Most of these groups were made up of part-time volunteers with military training and experience ranging from almost none to quite a bit. The rest of the units contained men who could be called "regulars" because they were willing to devote most or all of their time to soldiering. There were also a few small units of rangers, experienced frontier fighters who had long been protecting the settlements from Indians and pirates.

Overall, the members of these units were a mixed lot. Some were Anglo or Tejano Texians who had lived in Texas for several years, and others were Americans who had just moved to Texas. Among those later transplants were a few recent immigrants from European countries, including England, France,

In late December 1835 Santa Anna's army marched on the Texas territory with an army of six thousand men, as depicted in this scene from the 2004 film The Alamo.

Germany, and Denmark. Wherever they happened to be from, their motives varied. A number of the new arrivals agreed with the Texians' politics and wanted to help their cause. Others were frontiersmen simply looking for adventure or a good fight.

To their credit, nearly all the men in these assorted fighting groups were either enthusiastic about the revolution or tough, effective fighters—or both. However, they faced some serious problems and disadvantages that had to be overcome before the rebellion could succeed. First, their numbers were far fewer than those that Santa Anna, a national leader, could potentially raise. Second, the Texian military units were spread

The American defenders of the Alamo were a ragtag group of volunteers whose military training ranged from extensive to almost none.

A Desperate Need for Soldiers and Equipment

After General Cos surrendered at San Antonio, the Texians hoped that their victory there would send a signal to Santa Anna that they would not be intimidated by threats. Yet many of the Texian patriots were worried that they might not have enough soldiers and weapons to defeat a large Mexican army in open battle. Travis pointed out the difficulties involved in raising soldiers and war materials in a January 28, 1836, letter to Henry Smith, the governor of the Texian revolutionaries. "I have done everything in my power to get ready to march," Travis said.

But owing to the difficulty of getting horses, provisions, etc., and owing to desertions, etc., I shall march today with only about thirty men . . . [moreover] I have barely been able to get horses and equipment for the few men I have. . . . You have no idea of [the] exhausted state of this country. Volunteers can no longer be had or relied upon. A speedy organization, classification, and draft of the militia is all that can save us now. A regular army is necessary—but money, and money only, can raise and equip a regular army. Money must be raised or Texas has gone to ruin.

Quoted in Todd Hansen, ed. *The Alamo Reader: A Study in History.* Mechanicsburg, PA: Stackpole, 2003, p. 17.

far and wide and could not easily be brought together in one place. Third, they were largely disorganized, as a centralized military authority was still in the formative stages.

Finally, the volunteers, regulars, rangers, and others had no standardized outfits, gear, and weapons. This made supplying them and replacing their losses difficult. Texian Noah Smithwick penned a description of his fellow volunteer fighters as they looked in late 1835. "Words are inadequate to convey an impression of the appearance of the first Texas army as it formed in marching order," he began.

Buckskin breeches were the nearest approach to uniform and there was wide diversity even there, [as] some of them bring new and soft and yellow [buckskins], while others, from long familiarity with rain and grease and dirt, had become hard and black and shiny. . . . Here a broad brimmed sombrero [Mexican-style hat] overshadowed the military cap at its side; [and] a bulky roll of bed quilts jostled a pair of [store-bought] blankets . . . [and] the shaggy brown buffalo robe contrasted with a gaily colored checkered counterpane [bedspread] on which the manufacturer had lavished all the skill of dye and weave known to art. . . . [It was] a fantastic military array to a casual observer, but the one great purpose animating every heart clothed us in a uniform more perfect in our eyes than was ever donned by regular [soldiers] on dress parade.[32]

The Provisional Government

By the time Santa Anna organized his invasion forces in January 1836, the Texian rebels had been working on the problem of centralized organization and leadership for several months. Major headway was made in November 1835 while Austin was besieging Cos and his forces in San Antonio de Bexar. A convention, or meeting, of delegates from the major Texian towns began on November 3 in San Felipe de Austin, 153 miles (246km) east of San Antonio.

These men hotly debated whether Texas should remain part of Mexico or declare itself independent. Not surprisingly, members of the war party argued for independence, while those in the peace party wanted Texas to stay in the Mexican fold. By November 7 a compromise was reached whereby Texas would remain part of Mexico but would become a separate state in its own right. The 1824 Constitution had made Texas part of the larger state of Coahuila y Tejas, which was ruled largely by its local governor and legislature. Then in October 1835 Santa Anna had abolished the state governments and replaced them with fed-

eral districts called departments. Texas had become the department of Tejas, ruled directly by the dictator in Mexico City.

Such an arrangement was absolutely out of the question, the Texian delegates decided. So that same day (November 7, 1835) they declared Tejas to be the Mexican state of Texas and issued a statement that read in part, "The good People of Texas, availing themselves of their natural rights, solemnly declare, first, that they have taken up arms in defense of their rights and liberties, which were threatened by the encroachments of military despots, and in defense of the republican principles of the Federal Constitution of Mexico of 1824."[33]

Further, the document asserted, the Texians did not recognize the present authority in Mexico, that is, Santa Anna, although he was not specifically named. Nor would they lay down their arms as long as that renegade authority was on Texas soil and threatening the state and its citizens. The delegates also set up a provisional state government composed of a governor and a council of advisers. Henry Smith, from Velasco (on the Brazos River near the Gulf of Mexico coast), was elected governor.

Enter Sam Houston

In addition, Sam Houston was appointed commander in chief of the Provisional Army of Texas. A former governor of Tennessee, he had settled in Texas in 1833 and rapidly gotten involved in local politics. His post as head of the Provisional Army gave him no authority over

UNANIMOUS

DECLARATION OF INDEPENDENCE,

BY THE

DELEGATES OF THE PEOPLE OF TEXAS,

IN GENERAL CONVENTION,

AT THE TOWN OF WASHINGTON,

ON THE SECOND DAY OF MARCH, 1836.

The Texas Declaration of Independence was signed on March 6, 1836.

the units of volunteers led by Austin in San Antonio. Rather, Houston's task was to raise twenty-five hundred full-time soldiers from scratch and to pay them with land grants.

To that end, the new commander in chief wasted no time. Only a bit more than a month later, on December 12, 1835, Houston published a proclamation announcing the formation of a formal

How Houston Came to Texas

S am Houston, who played a pivotal role in the Texas Revolution, was born in 1793 in Virginia. His family moved to Tennessee when he was fourteen, and not long afterward he lived among the Cherokee Indians for three years. As a young man he served with future president Andrew Jackson in the wars fought between the U.S. Army and Creek Indians. Living with the Cherokee and fighting against the Creek gave Houston a healthy respect for Native Americans. So when the government began its brutal policy of Indian removal, he quit the military and established a law practice. That soon led to involvement in politics, and between 1819 and the late 1820s, he served as attorney general of Tennessee, as well as a U.S. representative from and governor of that state. In 1833 Andrew Jackson, who was then president, sent him to

negotiate with some Indians in Texas. Houston was so taken with the beauty of the region that he decided to settle down there, and he soon became involved in the local revolutionary movement.

Sam Houston was given the task of raising, training, and paying a twenty-five-hundred-man army to fight Santa Anna.

Texian army. Any man who joined for a minimum of two years or the duration of the war, it said, would receive 800 acres (323.75ha) of land, along with immediate citizenship in Texas. Houston also established an auxiliary unit of volunteers to supplement the main army. Members of the auxiliary force would each get 640 acres (259ha) of land if they fought for two years and 320 acres (129.5ha) if they served for only one year.

Finally, Houston made some military changes and appointments that ended up having major effects on how the events of the revolution, including the Alamo siege, unfolded. In particular, on December 21, 1835, he placed a talented artillery officer in charge of what had been, and would be again, a key location in the struggle—San Antonio. That officer, James C. Neill, originally from Alabama, was a hard worker and capable organizer who got along well with and inspired the soldiers under him.

These qualities immediately came in handy in a troubling situation that materialized in that same month and lingered into January 1836. In a nutshell, some of the men running Texas's new provisional government argued among themselves and became disorganized and inefficient. This caused discouragement among many Texian soldiers, some of whom left their posts and returned to their homes.

Yet notably, this did not happen at San Antonio, because Neill consistently kept up his men's spirits and raised their morale. Upon visiting the town on January 19, Jim Bowie was so impressed that he told Governor Smith in a letter, "All I can say of the soldiers stationed here is complimentary to both their courage and their patience. . . . I cannot eulogize [praise] the conduct and character of Col. Neill too highly. No other man in the army could have kept men at this post, [considering] the neglect they have [recently] experienced."[34]

A Natural Fort

Neill's accomplishments in San Antonio turned out to be fortunate, because the town became more strategically important as time progressed. At first, Houston and Bowie had given thought to abandoning it, reasoning that it would be too difficult to defend with its small group of volunteer soldiers. Houston had even suggested blowing up the Alamo mission just before leaving, because its large, walled enclosure made it such an effective fort. Without that stronghold, if the Mexicans took the town they would have a much harder time turning it into an effective defensive position.

This attitude changed, however, after Bowie's visit began on January 19. Both he and Neill concluded that leaving the town to the enemy would not be so smart after all. If Santa Anna did opt to invade Texas with a large army, a better strategy would be to keep him preoccupied in one place while the military units in the other towns prepared to attack him. As for that place, Neill and Bowie said, San Antonio was the most logical choice. There, the Texians, rather than the Mexicans, would benefit from the Alamo's qualities as a natural fort.

The Alamo's qualities as a natural fort made it the ideal place to keep Santa Anna's army occupied while the rest of Texas prepared an army to oppose him.

This reasoning was almost simultaneously reinforced by the arrival of reports from the south about Santa Anna's approach. In a letter to the provisional government, Bowie warned, "Santa Anna has arrived at Saltillo with [thousands of] troops," and "there are at the town of Rio Grande sixteen hundred more."[35] In a separate message, sent later, Bowie recommended that both the town and the Alamo be fortified the best way possible in anticipation of the Mexican army's arrival. It seemed certain, he said,

that an attack is shortly to be made on this place, and I think, and it is the general opinion [of my comrades], that the enemy will come by land [and march right through this region]. [Also] Col. Neill and myself have come to the solemn resolution that we will rather die in these ditches than give [San Antonio] up to the enemy. These citizens deserve our protection and the public safety demands our lives rather than to evacuate this post to the enemy.[36]

Travis and Bowie in Command

Another fortunate military decision that ended up molding the fate of this strategic Texas town was made by Smith. He ordered cavalry officer William Barret Travis to recruit some extra volunteers and take them to reinforce Neill in San Antonio. A native of South Carolina, Travis had moved to Texas in 1831 and established a law practice in Anahuac. He also became active in local politics and went on to become a member of the war party and an ardent supporter of independence for Texas. As an officer he was known for his serious manner, flair for the dramatic, and fearlessness.

Travis reached San Antonio on February 3, 1836, and soon found himself in the proverbial right place at the right time. A few days later Neill received word of some seriously ill family members in his hometown of Bastrop (north of Gonzales). Hurriedly resigning as San Antonio's commander, he left Travis in charge.

On February 14 Travis and Bowie agreed to share command. Bowie took charge of the volunteers, and Travis assumed leadership of the regulars. The

General William Travis drills his Texas fighters at the Alamo. On February 14, 1836, Travis and Bowie agreed to jointly command the Alamo's forces.

two men complemented each other, partly because they were both natural, strong, and courageous leaders. One prominent Texian later wrote, "Bowie was a born leader, never needlessly spending a bullet or imperiling a life. His voice is still ringing in my old deaf ears as he repeatedly admonished [cautioned] us: 'Keep under cover boys and reserve your fire; we haven't a man to spare.'"[37]

A Legendary Frontiersman

Not long before Travis and Bowie assumed joint command, a third born leader arrived in San Antonio. He was Davy Crockett, a name destined to live on with theirs as future generations remembered these men as the three most famous Alamo defenders. Born in Tennessee in 1786, Crockett had been a soldier under General Andrew Jackson (during the war between the U.S. Army and the Creek Indians), a legendary frontiersman, and a member of the U.S. Congress from 1829 to 1833.

After losing his reelection bid, Crockett became restless and decided to join the "gone to Texas" crowd. Departing Tennessee in late 1835, he reached San Augustine, in eastern Texas, on January 9, 1836. That same day he wrote a message to his son and daughter to tell them about his arrival and high hopes for thriving in Texas. At the time he had no way of knowing it would be the last letter he ever penned. "I have got through safe, and have been received by everybody with the open arm of friendship," he wrote.

I would be glad to see every friend I have settle [here]. It would be a fortune to them all. I have taken the oath of the Government [a vow of loyalty taken by all Texians at the time], and have enrolled my name as a volunteer [in the Texian militia] for six months, and will set out for the Rio Grande in a few days. . . . I am rejoiced at my fate. I had rather be in my present situation than to be elected to a seat in Congress for life. I am in hopes of making a fortune for myself and family.[38]

No sooner had Crockett joined the militia than he was called to action. On January 13 he and about a dozen other military volunteers left for southern Texas, where, it was well known, trouble with the Mexicans was brewing. They rode into San Antonio on February 8 and offered their services to the garrison commanders.

No Time Left

Neill (who had not yet taken his leave) and Travis welcomed the newcomers and put them to work with the other defenders, stockpiling provisions and beefing up fortifications. Neill, Travis, and Bowie were all confident the defenses would be ready by the time the Mexican army arrived, because they believed the army was still at least a few weeks away. The assumption was that Santa Anna would wait for early spring. That way his cavalry horses and pack animals would have sufficient grasses for grazing.

Famed Tennessee frontiersman Davy Crockett moved to Texas in 1836 and almost immediately volunteered his services at the Alamo.

But this turned out to be nothing more than wishful thinking. The reality was that Mexico's dictator had driven his soldiers hard in a forced march, and they were now a good deal closer than the Texians thought. The vanguard, or leading elements, of the Mexican army reached the Alazan Creek, only a few miles from San Antonio, on the morning of February 23, 1836. When some friendly Tejanos reported this fact to Travis, he was at first skeptical. So he sent two scouts on horseback to check it out. A few minutes later they came riding back at full speed, and Travis realized the awful truth. A sentry in the town's church tower rang the large bell that hung there to alert and assemble the soldiers and citizens

At that critical moment, Travis and Bowie realized there was no time left to complete the defenses they had planned for the town. So they ordered the garrison to move into the Alamo, on which they had recently made several repairs. The mission-fort consisted of a rectangular central courtyard, or plaza, a bit more than one and a half football fields in extent. Much of its perimeter was lined with one- or two-story adobe houses, a long army barracks built earlier by Mexican garrisons, some horse and cattle pens, and an old church with very thick, sturdy adobe walls. Most of these structures were connected to a protective outer wall with a main gate in its south section.

There was, however, one glaring weak spot—a 60-foot gap (18m) in the east wall that left the compound wide open to entry by an enemy. "To span the gap," scholar William C. Davis says,

Travis and his Texians built a stockade fence "with a ditch on the outer side, and beyond that . . . tree limbs buried in the ground with their sharpened branches pointing in the direction from which an attacker would come."[39] The defenders also placed a cannon on the enclosure's northwest corner, another on the southwest corner, and three more atop the church's roof. They put their last two cannons in the horse and cattle pens.

Travis and Bowie knew that to defend the Alamo properly would have required at least five hundred soldiers. For now, however, there was no choice but to do the best they could with the roughly 150 men they had. Their fervent hope was that reinforcements would arrive soon. Houston might send them. Or they might come from James Fannin, who now oversaw upward of four hundred fighters in the Texian fort at Goliad, 90 miles (145km) southeast of San Antonio.

While his people were entering the Alamo, Travis scribbled a plea for aid reading: "The enemy in large force is in sight. We [need] men and provisions. Send them to us. We have 150 men and are determined to defend the garrison to the last."[40] At that moment, he had no way of knowing how prophetic the words *to the last* would turn out to be.

Chapter Four

The Alamo Is Surrounded and Besieged

"I will never forget how that army looked as it swept into town," eighty-eight-year-old Juan Diaz wrote in 1907, remembering a haunting image from his youth. In 1836 Diaz, then sixteen, was a Tejano resident of San Antonio de Bexar. His father was the custodian of the local San Fernando Church. On February 23, hearing the sound of a band playing in the distance, the curious youth climbed the winding stairs leading to the tower of his father's church. There he could clearly see the arrival of the Mexican army, with its columns of neatly uniformed soldiers stretching all the way back to the horizon. His recollection continued:

> At the head of the soldiers came the regimental band, playing the liveliest airs [tunes], and with the band came a squad of men bearing the flags and banners of Mexico and an immense image that looked like an alligator's head. The band stopped on [the town's] Main Plaza [and next came many cannons, which] had a clean sweep to the Alamo, for at the time there were no buildings between it and the San Fernando [church].[41]

Diaz was not the only spectator of this event and those of the fateful days that followed. Other local Tejanos of various ages, as well as a number of Santa Anna's soldiers and officers, witnessed and later described bits and pieces of the Alamo siege, which lasted thirteen days. From February 23 to March 5, 1836, Santa Anna's army surrounded, blockaded, and prepared to capture the mission-fort. The sights and sounds of the booming cannons, massed musket fire, flashing swords, galloping horses' hooves, and human agony were forever burned into the memories of those who were there and survived to tell their tales.

A Fight to the Death

Some of those survivors, including Diaz, watched the Mexican troops scurrying through the streets, rapidly reclaiming the town. A group of soldiers set up cannons and other large guns in the main plaza, while others prepared for the arrival of Santa Anna and the rest of the army. The dictator arrived sometime in the afternoon.

Eight-year-old Enrique Esparza, son of one of the Alamo's Tejano defenders, later remembered details of Santa Anna's entry. The use of this testimony, along with that of Diaz and other bystanders and participants, demonstrates how historians benefit greatly from eyewitness accounts to help them piece together long-ago events. "I saw Santa Anna when he arrived," Esparza later said.

I saw him dismount. He did not hitch his horse [to a wooden rail in the customary manner]. He proceeded immediately to the house on the northwest corner of Main Plaza. I was playing with some other children on the plaza and when Santa Anna and his soldiers came up, we ran up and told our parents, who almost immediately

This map of the Alamo environs is based on Santa Anna's original battlefield map of the siege.

afterward took me and the other children of the family to the Alamo. I am sure of this, for I saw Santa Anna several times afterward and after I came out of the Alamo.[42]

Very soon after the Mexican supreme commander's entry into the town, a cannon fired to herald the event. Then Santa Anna had some soldiers raise a red flag high enough for the Texians in the Alamo to see clearly. A young Tejano carpenter named Pablo Diaz was watching all this intently and later explained the flag's dark and frightening significance: "I heard the gun fired from the plaza and saw the [red] flag floating [there]. When Santa Anna hoisted [it], it was his announcement that no quarter [leniency or mercy] would be shown those opposing him. This was well understood by those in the Alamo. They knew that unless Houston . . . sent them succor [assistance] they were lost."[43]

Santa Anna also ordered a company of buglers standing in the plaza to play the *deguello*. This tune was widely dreaded in Spanish and Mexican warfare. The word means "slit throat," and the buglers played it to signify that no mercy would be given in the ensuing conflict. It would be a grim and uncompromising fight to the death.

Santa Anna's Strategy

In fact, from their vantages atop the Alamo's walls and rooftops, the defenders saw the red flag and heard the *deguello*'s ominous strains echoing in the distance. William Barret Travis took these events exactly as they were intended—as a threat. So he responded in a way he and his compatriots saw as appropriate: with a short barrage of cannon fire. Evidence shows that it killed one Mexican and injured about eight others. In retaliation, Santa Anna fired some of his own big guns at the fort, but these volleys had no effect.

Despite this aggressive exchange of armaments, Jim Bowie somehow thought he had earlier seen the Mexicans signal a desire for agents from the two sides to talk before fighting. So without consulting Travis, he sent Major Green Jameson under a flag of truce to discuss possible surrender terms. Jameson met with some Mexican officers, who basically said the defenders' lives would be spared if they threw themselves on Santa Anna's mercy. The exact words, spoken to Jameson by one of Santa Anna's personal aides, Colonel Batres (also sometimes spelled Bartres), were:

I reply to you, according to the order of his Excellency [the president, that is, Santa Anna], that the Mexican army cannot come to terms under any conditions with rebellious foreigners to whom there is no recourse left. If they wish to save their lives, [they must] place themselves immediately at the disposal of [Santa Anna], from whom alone they may expect clemency [mercy] after some considerations.[44]

Bowie's precise reaction to these remarks is unknown. But it is likely

Crockett Greets the Defenders

According to tradition, when Davy Crockett arrived in San Antonio, his first words were, "Where's the action?" But like so many other words and actions credited to him over the years, these were likely fabricated later. What has been firmly documented is a short speech he gave to the town's defenders, whose spirits were raised by the arrival of such a well-known American. "Fellow citizens, I am among you," he told them. "I have come to aid you all that I can in your noble cause. I shall identify myself with your interest, and all the honor that I desire is that of defending . . . in common with my fellow citizens, the liberties of our common country." The speech clearly reveals that, like many others in those days, Crockett firmly equated the Texian cause of liberty and independence with American political ideals and territorial interests.

Quoted in Paul Robert Walker. *Remember the Alamo: Texians, Tejanos, and Mexicans Tell Their Stories*. Washington, DC: National Geographic Society, 2007, p. 34.

he found them more than a little contradictory. If it was possible that Santa Anna might show mercy and spare the defenders' lives, why had he so blatantly raised the red flag and ordered his buglers to sound the *deguello*?

At least some indication of what Santa Anna was actually thinking at that moment can be seen in his surviving memoirs. He described how the "rebel settlers" retreated from the town into "Fort Alamo, which they had well fortified." Then he called them "traitors" who "shall never again occupy" San Antonio. Next he bragged about how he had forced the enemy to cower so badly that "they are not even allowed to raise their heads over the walls." Finally, Santa Anna said he was "preparing everything" for an "assault" on the Alamo. "Up to now they act stubbornly, counting on the strong position which they hold, and hoping for much aid from their colonies . . . but they shall soon find out their mistake."[45]

Thus, the Mexican dictator's intentions appear fairly clear. He did not want to negotiate with or forgive those inside the Alamo. Rather, he planned to surround and capture the fort and then severely punish those inside, along with other Texian rebels. As for his overall strategy, his own account and those of some of his officers show that he first intended to seal off the Alamo from the outside world. That way the defenders would receive no supplies or reinforcements, so the process of wearing them down would be quicker.

That process, which began only hours after the Mexicans entered San Antonio, would be accomplished in large part by bombarding the fort with cannonballs for extended periods each day and sometimes at night. Also, Santa Anna's men would dig a series of trenches outside the Alamo, mostly during the night so the defenders could not see what was happening. Each night new trenches would be created closer to the structure than the existing ones. Over the course of days, the Mexicans would lower some of their cannons into these trenches, moving the artillery closer and closer to the walls, so as to cause them ever more damage.

"Victory or Death!"

When the sun rose on the siege's second day, February 24, 1836, units of the Mexican army began to implement the first part of Santa Anna's plan—surrounding the Alamo. This entailed having small units scout the area and find the best places to put soldiers and cannons. This

Santa Anna had no intentions of negotiating with the Alamo defenders. He planned to surround and capture the fort and severely punish those inside.

process had to be carried out with caution. The troops had to be stationed close enough to both contain and intimidate the defenders, but not so close that they might be picked off by Texian sharpshooters.

While this was happening well outside the Alamo's walls, inside the Texians continued their preparations for the siege. For instance, they secured the wives and children of some of the defenders in the main room and other chambers of the church. Among them were Enrique Esparza's mother, brother, and sister. There, too, Susannah Dickenson, wife of artillery officer Almeron Dickenson, and their fifteen-month-old daughter, Angelina, found temporary residence. The men also worked to improve the cannon placements and to pile up earthen barriers to protect the entrances to the buildings facing the central plaza.

During a long break Travis took from supervising these efforts, he penned another request for help, this one destined to become a world-famous expression of the human desire for freedom. "To the people of Texas and all Americans in the world," it began.

I am besieged by a thousand or more of the Mexicans under Santa Anna. I have sustained a continued bombardment for twenty-four hours, and have not lost a man. The enemy have demanded a surrender at discretion; otherwise the garrison is to be put to the sword if the place is taken. . . . I shall never surrender or retreat. Then I call on you in the name of liberty, of patriotism, and of everything dear to the American character, to come to our aid with all dispatch, [for] the enemy are receiving reinforcements daily. . . . Though this call may be neglected, I am determined to sustain myself as long as possible, and die like a soldier who never forgets what is due to his own honor and that of his country. Victory or death![46]

That evening, Captain Albert Martin, who had been a store owner before joining the Texian army, bravely galloped his horse through the Mexican lines and delivered the message to the revolutionary authorities in Gonzales.

As if Travis were not under enough pressure as co-commander of the Alamo garrison, that same day he suddenly found himself its lone leader. Bowie had been feeling unwell for several days, but in a brave effort to carry out his duties had managed to shrug off his discomfort. Suddenly, however, he collapsed and was carried to a makeshift hospital inside the barracks. The exact nature of his illness remains a matter of debate. Some modern experts think it was typhoid fever, as did many of those in the Alamo. Others have suggested it was pneumonia or tuberculosis. What is certain is that with Bowie out of commission, Travis was now in charge of everyone in the fort.

Bowie's condition was serious enough that he was drifting in and out of consciousness for the rest of the afternoon and evening. So he did not hear the racket that kept most of the rest of the defenders awake and tense. It was another aspect of the enemy's strategy, as recalled later by Mexican cavalry officer Rafael Saldana. "One of the measures [we] employed," he wrote,

was that of constant alarms during the hours of the night. At intervals, when silence reigned over the Alamo and all was still in camp, the artillery would open [fire], a great shout would be raised by the besieging forces, and this uproar . . . was intended to make the impression that a night assault had been planned, and also to make it appear to the [Texians] that their expected reinforcements, while trying to make their way into the Alamo, had become engaged with the enemy and were being destroyed.[47]

William Travis's famed "Victory or Death" statement penned from the Alamo. In it Travis vowed to fight to the last man—a vow he would keep.

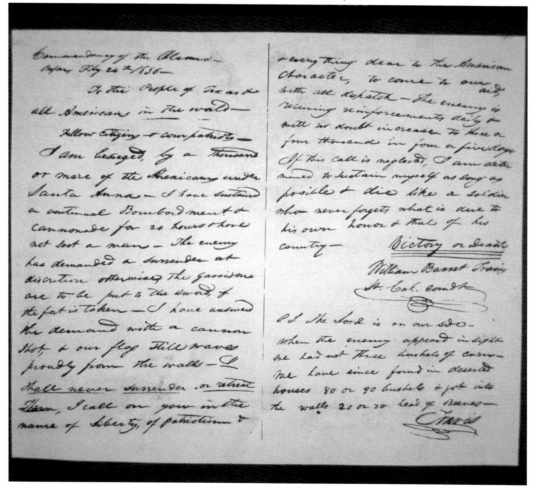

The Weapons of the Day

The Texians and Mexicans who fought in San Antonio in the mid-1830s used the most common armaments of that era. The biggest and most destructive weapons of the day were artillery pieces, or cannons, some of which could fire projectiles hundreds of yards. The different types of cannon were defined by the weights of the cannonballs they fired. A piece that used an 8-pound (3.6kg) ball, for instance, was called an "eight-pounder." Nearly all the artillery pieces employed in the Alamo siege were eight-, ten-, or twelve-pounders. In addition, individual soldiers most often used the musket, or flintlock, an early firearm invented by the Spanish in the 1500s. The first step in loading a musket was to pour gunpowder down the front barrel. The operator then inserted a small lead ball into the barrel. When the trigger was pulled, a small metal knob called the hammer struck a piece of flint, which gave off a spark that in turn ignited the powder in the barrel. That small but forceful explosion pushed the ball outward toward the intended target. Hitting that target was no easy task, however, as muskets were not very accurate. They also took a long time to load. Among the other weapons of the day were swords, knives, and bayonets, all used in close combat. Cavalrymen, or horsemen, also used swords, along with lances, long spears with which they often impaled soldiers running on foot.

The Alamo defenders used flintlock muskets, as well as cannons to defend the mission.

Battle for the Huts

The next day, February 25, was a tense and busy one for the defenders. The Mexican cannons began firing at the mission early, and a little while later the Texian sentries saw a force of at least two hundred Mexicans crossing the San Antonio River in the distance. These troops then made their way to a small group of thatched-roof huts situated fewer than 600 feet (183m) from the Alamo's southwestern corner.

This was too close for comfort for Travis. Running up onto the wooden platform his men had constructed as a cannon bastion on that corner of the compound, he shouted for his best riflemen to gather there. A few minutes later, at his order, they opened fire on the huts to keep the Mexicans hiding in them pinned down. Meanwhile, Travis had the operators of the cannon beside him target the huts, too.

For a solid two hours, the Texian barrage pounded the enemy position, while in opposition Mexican cannons continued to target the fort. During this stressful period, Travis was relieved to see that none of his soldiers were hit by the incoming missiles. He was also pleased at his men's upbeat attitude and determination in the face of dire danger. "Both officers and men conducted themselves with firmness and bravery,"[48] he later wrote.

Particularly helpful was Davy Crockett, as always a natural leader with a knack for knowing what to do in a crisis. Travis noted how "the Hon[orable] David Crockett was seen at all points,

animating the men to do their duty."[49] Enrique Esparza later recalled Crockett's antics, saying that he "seemed everywhere. He could shoot from the wall or through the portholes [the men had drilled here and there to shoot through]. Then he would run back and say something funny. He tried to speak Spanish sometimes. Now and then he would run to the fire we had in the courtyard . . . to make us laugh."[50]

Finally, the Mexicans who had taken over the huts could bear no more, and they suddenly bolted. Grabbing his spyglass, Travis watched them retreat, and he estimated they were carrying a minimum of eight dead or wounded comrades. As soon as the enemy had moved far enough away, he asked for a team of volunteers to run out to the huts and burn them. Several men stepped forward to take on this task, which they completed before the Mexicans could muster a unit of soldiers to stop them.

Reinforcements at Last

The fourth day of the siege, February 26, began with a cold winter chill blowing in from the north, making the soldiers in both armies miserable. Nevertheless, they were often on the move. The sun was barely up when a Texian lookout noticed a small unit of General Sesma's cavalry riding from west to east in the distance. In a bold move, at Travis's order several horsemen from the Alamo galloped out and attacked the Mexican riders. The skirmish did not last long, however. The well-trained Mexican cavalrymen rapidly gained the upper hand,

and they promptly drove the Texians back to the fort. Travis was thankful that none of his men were injured in the scuffle.

This was not the only outside foray attempted by the Texians that day. In addition, several small parties of defenders slipped out to look for firewood. In his account of the siege, Santa Anna's chief of staff, Juan Almonte, said the foragers also appeared to be searching for water sources. But though it cannot be ruled out, this is not likely. The Texians had by this time dug a well inside the Alamo, and all indications are that they had sufficient water supplies throughout the siege.

Saturday, February 27, and Sunday, February 28, 1836, were notable for a valiant but failed attempt to reinforce the beleaguered Alamo defenders. At Goliad, James Fannin at last felt his own soldiers were ready to go to the aid of their fellow Texians. With more than three hundred men, along with four cannons carried on large wagons, the relief force set out on Saturday morning.

A mere two hours into the march, however, three of the wagons broke down. Moreover, when the expedition reached the San Antonio River, the oxen were unable to drag the cannons across. At the end of the day, the Goliad contingent had traveled a paltry half a mile, and the exhausted men camped for the night. On Sunday morning they discovered to their dismay that most of the oxen and horses had wandered off. After meeting with

his officers, Fannin regretfully made the only realistic decision he could—to return to Goliad.

However, the Alamo defenders did finally receive reinforcements, even if the numbers were not as high as had been hoped. During the night of March 1, thirty-two volunteers from Gonzales entered the Alamo, increasing the garrison's strength to 187. "Most of the Mexican patrols had been concentrating on [guarding] the road to Goliad," Tim J. Todish and Terry S. Todish explain, "and the volunteers were able to make it through undetected." But there was a slight hitch. "Around 3:00 A.M., just as they thought they had reached the fort safely, a nervous Texian sentry fired on them and wounded one of the men in the foot. The indignant outburst that followed left no doubt that the shadows in the dark were friends, and the 'Immortal 32' [as they later came to be called] were welcomed into the Alamo without further incident."[51]

Fighting a Monster

The next day, March 2, witnessed both sides unable to compose any messages. This was due to a cold snap so severe that ink froze solid in the inkwells. Not surprisingly, the soldiers of the two armies huddled around their fires, doing their best to stay warm, and no fighting took place.

Nevertheless, it turned out to be a fateful day in Texas history. Unbeknownst to both the Alamo defenders and their nemesis Santa Anna, miles away in Washington-on-the Brazos more than fifty Texian leaders, including Sam Houston, took drastic action. Fed up with what they saw as Santa Anna's tyranny, they stated in writing, "The people of Texas, in solemn convention assembled . . . do hereby resolve and declare, that our political connection with the Mexican nation has forever ended, and that the people of Texas do now constitute a free, sovereign, and independent republic, and are fully invested with all the rights and attributes which properly belong to independent nations."[52]

On March 3 the temperature moderated enough for ink to flow once more, and Travis penned a few more messages to the outside world. In one he said, "I have held this place 10 days against a force variously estimated from 1,500 to 6,000. . . . We are ready to peril our lives a hundred times a day, and to drive away the monster who is fighting us under a blood-red flag, threatening to murder all prisoners and make Texas a waste desert. . . . If my countrymen do not rally to my relief, I am determined to perish in the defense of this place."[53]

No more relief was forthcoming, however. At least for the moment, therefore, the defenders were on their own. This did not bode well for them because the next day, March 4, Santa Anna met with his senior officers to discuss a major attack on the Alamo.

Travis did not know about the meeting, of course. But it appears that he sensed that such an assault was coming. On March 5, the thirteenth day of

Legend says that Alamo commander William Travis drew a line in the sand and asked all those willing to stay and fight to step over it.

the siege, he called all his men together and told them there was no hope that any more reinforcements would come in the near future. He had decided to stay, he said. But anyone who desired to leave was free to do so. Tradition claims he drew a line in the sand and asked all those who were willing to stay to step over it.

Historians point out that this event, though possible, cannot be documented for certain. What seems sure is that all but one of the defenders agreed to stay and fight. The single exception, Frenchman Louis Rose, waited for dark, quietly slipped over the wall, and crept through the enemy lines to safety.

An hour or two later, at 10:00 P.M., the Mexican cannons, which had been belching fire and smoke all day, suddenly went silent. The Alamo defenders decided this would be an opportune time to catch a badly needed nap. At that moment they had no way of knowing that they had fewer than nine hours left to live.

Chapter Five

The Final Assault and the Alamo's Fall

Early in the bleak, overcast morning of March 6, 1836, after thirteen days of nearly continuous cannon barrage, Santa Anna launched an all-out attack on the Alamo. He was banking on the element of surprise. The fort's defenders must be exhausted from getting so little sleep during the siege, he reasoned. His order to halt the cannon bombardment at ten o'clock the night before had taken advantage of that fact. In the quiet hours that followed, the Texians would surely try get in some badly needed shut-eye. So the dictator timed the attack to begin before dawn, when the defenders would likely be dozing and unprepared to meet a sudden, large-scale assault on the walls.

To surmount those walls, the Mexican soldiers would use wooden scaling ladders. Their orders, once they had made it inside the compound, were to slay every man they saw, even those who surrendered. "Santa Anna declared that none should survive," reported Colonel Fernando Urizza in an account penned years later. Urizza served as Santa Anna's secretary during the late-night meetings in which the dictator and his officers planned the attack. General Manuel Castrillón tried to persuade the president "to spare the lives of the [Texian] men," Urizza recalled.

Santa Anna was holding in his hand the leg of a chicken which he was eating, and holding it up, he said: "What are the lives of soldiers more than of so many chickens? I tell you, the Alamo must fall, and my orders must be obeyed at all hazards. If our soldiers are driven back, the next line in their rear must force those before them forward, and compel them to scale the walls, cost what it may.[54]

These words showed not only contempt for the enemy, but also a disregard for the lives of the Mexican soldiers. This made many of Santa Anna's officers, who had risen through the ranks under more humane commanders, very uncomfortable. Especially troubling was the order to take no prisoners. The officers had no qualms about killing the enemy during the assault, as that was expected in wartime. However, to slay even those who surrendered struck them as unethical,

Mexican commander Santa Anna ordered that no prisoners be taken at the Alamo; they were all to be killed whether they surrendered or not.

even uncivilized. The problem was that the officers feared for their own lives if they refused to follow the dictator's orders. Urizza, Castrillón, and the others knew they faced a long, frustrating night in which doing their jobs would be complicated by no small amount of soul searching.

The Attack Begins

From these officers, the orders telling how to prosecute the attack filtered down through the chain of command. Mexican sergeant Manuel Loranca later recalled how he quietly briefed the infantrymen in his charge during the dark initial hours of March 6. By around three o'clock in the morning, he said, "The Mexican infantry, with ladders, were lying down at musket-shot distance [from the Alamo's walls], awaiting the signal of assault."[55]

One of those soldiers resting on his stomach on the cold ground near the fort was an unidentified Mexican infantryman who later wrote:

> I was under the orders of General Cos and therefore will relate what I saw at close range. After a roundabout approach we stopped at 3:00 A.M. about 300 paces from the [northwest corner of] the enemy's fort. . . . We remained on the

Louis Rose's Little-Known Story

One of the most fascinating and least-known stories of the Alamo defenders is that of Louis Rose, one of the few firmly documented members of the original garrison to escape death. (The others were couriers Travis sent out with pleas for reinforcements.) Born in France in 1785, in 1806 Rose joined Napoléon Bonaparte's army and served with distinction in campaigns in Spain, Naples, and Russia. It remains unknown how Rose ended up in North America. But in 1827 he was working as a log cutter in a sawmill in eastern Texas. At some point he met and became friends with Jim Bowie, and evidently Bowie convinced him to join the soldiers who were besieging General Cos's forces in San Antonio in the autumn of 1835. A few months later, Rose was still in San Antonio and entered the Alamo with Bowie when the Mexican army arrived. Rose later said that when Travis drew a line in the sand and asked those who were willing to stay to cross it, he (Rose) decided not to do so. He felt it was not his fight, so that night he departed and managed to slip through the Mexican lines to safety. Whether or not it was deserved, thereafter Rose lived with the label of coward. He died in Louisiana in 1851.

ground until 5:30 (the morning felt quite cool), when the signal to march was given by his Excellency the President, from his battery situated to the northeast.[56]

The soldier told how Cos then shouted for the men in his column to jump to their feet. "We ran to the assault," the younger man remembered. "Ladders, beams, bars, pick axes, etc. were carried for that purpose." It was not far to the wall, he continued. But it was still dark out, so it was hard to see exactly what was happening. Also, the Texians fired a cannon at the column, killing at least forty of its members in the space of a few seconds. "The tenacious resistance of our enemy was to be admired," the solider recalled, as was

the dauntless steadiness of all the [Mexican] generals, chiefs, officers, and troops. It seemed as though the shot and bullets from the cannons, muskets, and rifles of the enemy found their mark on the chests of our soldiers, who ceaselessly shouted "Long Live the Mexican Republic!" "Long Live General Santa Anna!" I assure you that all signs of fear or terror disappeared at the sight of so many brave men [locked in mortal combat].[57]

The Alamo Awakens
Meanwhile, the scene within the Alamo was no less animated and dramatic once the defenders knew they were

under attack. However, it took them a few anxious moments to snap out of the drowsy state they had entered shortly before midnight the night before. William Barret Travis's slave and trusty companion, Joe, later described the lead-up to and first minutes of the attack from the Texian point of view: "On Saturday night, March 5, the little garrison had worked hard, in repairing and strengthening their position, until a late hour. And when the attack was made, which was just before daybreak, sentinels and all were asleep, except the officer of the day [the soldier temporarily in charge while Travis was asleep] who was just starting on his round."[58]

Besides the officer of the day, Captain John J. Baugh, the only other Texians who were supposed to be awake at that juncture were three picket guards whom Travis had placed outside the fortress. Their job was to remain watchful and alert the Alamo garrison if enemy soldiers tried to sneak up on them. According to Edwin P. Hoyt, however, the unfortunate pickets were "exhausted from night after night of wakefulness, watching, and listening. One by one they drifted off [to sleep] in their hiding places. Here, the enemy's scouts found them. A quick thrust with a knife and the pickets were put to sleep forever."[59]

That left Baugh the only person in the fort who was wide awake when Santa Anna gave the order to attack. The first realization Joe had of the oncoming danger came when Baugh burst into Travis's quarters and yelled, "The Mexicans are coming!"[60] The American army officer

The attack on the Alamo began just before dawn on March 6th with Mexican troops using scaling ladders to breach the mission walls.

who later wrote down Joe's account (because the slave was illiterate) said that the Mexicans

> were running at full speed with their scaling ladders towards the fort, and . . . had their ladders against the wall before the [Texians] were aroused to resistance. Travis sprung up, and seizing his rifle and sword, called to Joe to take his gun and [then Travis] mounted the wall and called out to his men, "Come on boys, the Mexicans are upon us, and we'll give them hell!" He immediately fired his rifle [and Joe fired his own gun].[61]

Trouble on the North Side

From their position atop the north wall, Travis and Joe gazed out into the pre-dawn darkness. Repeated flashes of light from the masses of firing muskets allowed them to make out the approaching enemy infantry. The initial Texian salvo made an enormous dent in those ranks because of their shape. "Unlike the Anglo-American tactic of advancing in a long line," a modern authority notes, "the Mexican army advanced in a French column formation, two companies wide, with the remainder of the assault force stretched out behind. Only the front two ranks could safely fire during the advance, and the tightly packed columns were perfect targets for both artillery and small-arms fire."[62]

As the Mexicans in the front ranks fell under the defenders' first barrage of gunfire, the next couple of ranks ran forward to the foot of the walls. There they were momentarily safe, unless a Texian took the chance of leaning over and firing straight downward at them. This is exactly what Travis did, Joe later testified. The Alamo's commander emptied his shotgun into a group of attackers below, and a second later another Mexican took advantage of the man's exposed position. A ball from a musket penetrated Travis's forehead, and his stiffened body tumbled downward from the battlement.

After Travis's demise, the north wall increasingly became the principal focus of the fighting. Santa Anna's original objective had been for columns of soldiers to assault the fort on all four sides at the same time. His officers executed that plan. But as the formations swayed to and fro in the darkness under a hail of Texian bullets, some of them steadily shifted toward the north, as later described by one of the Mexican soldiers.

> The three columns that attacked the west, the north, and the east fronts, fell back, or rather, wavered at the first discharge from the enemy. . . . The columns of the western and eastern attacks, meeting with some difficulties in reaching the tops of the small houses which formed the walls of the fort, did, by a simultaneous movement to the right and to the left, swing northward till the three columns formed one dense mass, which under the guidance of their officers, endeavored to climb the [wall] on that side.[63]

The nighttime assault on the Alamo from all sides is accurately depicted in this scene from the 2004 film The Alamo.

Death by Friendly Fire

Partly because so many of the attackers bunched together, and also due to the darkness and the sheer momentum of the moving columns, the Mexicans suffered badly from friendly fire. An unfortunate occurrence in all wars, this is the accidental killing of soldiers by their own comrades. Sergeant Loranca summed it up concisely, saying, "In the act of assault" on the north wall, "a confusion occurred, occasioned by darkness, in which the Mexican troops opened fire on each other."[64]

A more detailed account of the toll taken by friendly fire came later from one of the soldiers who actually fought in the congested mass of men pressing on the north wall. "Our loss was very heavy," the account begins.

Colonel Francisco Duque was mortally wounded at the very beginning. As he lay dying on the ground where he was being trampled by his own men, he still ordered them on to the slaughter. This attack was extremely injudicious [unwise] and in opposition to military rules, for our own men were exposed not only to the fire of the enemy but also to that of our own columns attacking the other fronts. And our soldiers being formed in close columns, all shots that were aimed too low, struck the backs of our foremost men. The greatest number of our casualties took place in that manner. It may even be affirmed that not one fourth of our wounded were struck by the enemy's fire.[65]

How Did Bowie Die?

The manner in which Jim Bowie died in the makeshift infirmary in the Alamo's barracks remains uncertain. Two alleged eyewitnesses later made claims about his death. But they contradicted each other, and one did not identify Bowie by name, so most historians have not fully accepted either account. One was that of a Mexican sergeant, Francisco Beccera. He said that when he entered the barracks, "I saw a man lying on a bed" who was "evidently sick." Although Santa Anna had ordered that all men inside the Alamo must be killed, Beccera could not bring himself to slay an unarmed invalid and began to leave. But then two other Mexican soldiers entered, and suddenly the prostrate man produced a pistol and shot them dead. At this, Beccera changed his mind. "I then fired and killed the Texian,"[1] he later testified, although he did not know whether the patient was Bowie or not. The second account was that of Madama Candelaria, a Tejano woman who had been caring for Bowie during most of the siege. She claimed that "Colonel Bowie died in my arms only a few minutes before the entrance to the Alamo by the [Mexican] soldiers. I was holding his [lifeless] hand in my lap when Santa Anna's men swarmed into the room."[2]

1. Quoted in Alan C. Huffines. *Blood of Noble Men: The Alamo Siege and Battle*. Austin, TX: Eakin, 2006, p. 158.
2. Quoted in Huffines. *Blood of Noble Men*, p. 168.

One account of the death of Jim Bowie had him shooting Mexican soldiers from his sickbed.

The Slaughter Inside

Despite the heavy casualties the attackers took outside the walls, their large numbers eventually allowed them to prevail. As more and more Texians atop the walls were killed, Mexican soldiers began pouring into the central plaza. In response, following Travis's prearranged plan, the surviving defenders swiftly fell back behind the earthen mounds they had placed in front of the entrances to the church and barracks. Some of them fired around those barriers, while others poked their gun barrels through holes they had earlier drilled in the adobe walls.

One of these men, Almeron Dickenson, hurried into the church's main room, where his frightened wife, Susannah, was clutching their baby daughter. "Great God, Sue!" he cried. "The Mexicans are inside our walls! All is lost! If they spare you, save my child!"[66] He quickly kissed her on lips, then turned and ran back into the fray. It was the last time she saw him alive.

Young Enrique Esparza was also in one of the inner chambers with his mother and siblings and later described the sounds of battle that drew ever closer to them.

> We could hear the Mexican officers shouting to the men to jump over, and the men were fighting so close that we could hear them strike each other. It was so dark that we couldn't see anything, and the families that were in the quarters just huddled up in the corners.

My mother's children were near her. Finally they began shooting through the dark into the room where we were. A boy who was wrapped in a blanket in one corner was hit and killed. The Mexicans fired into the room for at least fifteen minutes. It was a miracle, but none of [my family members] were touched.[67]

As the slaughter inside the Alamo continued, Mexican soldiers broke into rooms across the compound and shot or bayoneted nearly everyone they found. A few women and children were spared, partly because officers restrained their men from butchering unarmed civilians. Other Mexicans broke into the makeshift hospital in the barracks where Jim Bowie still lay on a cot. The exact manner of his death is unknown. Movies and other traditional versions usually show him emptying his pistols into the first two attackers and killing a few more with his huge knife before being overwhelmed. But it is also possible he was too weak to lift the knife or that he was already dead when the assault began.

Near the end of the battle, the Alamo's quartermaster, Eliel Melton, and roughly sixteen to twenty other defenders decided that further resistance was futile. Taking advantage of the darkness, they wove their way through the still oncoming Mexican lines and made a desperate escape attempt. Santa Anna had foreseen this possibility, however. He had stationed mounted lancers in the plain outside the fort, and they chased down and killed most of the fugitives. One escapee hid under a bush, but the lancers found and shot him.

There remains a slight possibility that one or two of the Texians in Melton's party managed to get away. For example, a man named Henry Warnell died three months later of injuries he said he sustained in the battle. But no reliable evidence has ever been found to prove he was actually at the Alamo.

The Crockett Death Controversy

By the time the escaped Texians met their end, most or all of the remaining defenders within the Alamo were dead as well. Some evidence suggests that Davy Crockett and the small band of men fighting around him were among the last to die. However, a tremendous amount of theorizing and controversy has surrounded Crockett's demise over the years. Some experts say that he likely died fighting, as both the slave Joe and Enrique Esparza claimed. "Crockett and a few of his friends were found together," Joe recalled, "with twenty-four of the enemy dead around them."[68] According to Esparza, "He clubbed his rifle when they closed in on him and knocked them down with its stock until he was overwhelmed by [their] numbers and slain. . . . When he died, there was a heap of slain [Mexicans] in front and on each side of him."[69]

However, a number of scholars support a claim made by several of the Mexican officers. (The most notable of their accounts is by Lieutenant José Enrique de la Peña.) They said that a few Texians were taken prisoner at the close of the battle and brought before Santa Anna. Angry that they had been allowed to live, he ordered their execution, which was immediately carried out. Supposedly, Davy Crockett was a member of this group.

Those historians who doubt this claim argue that its presentation in the Mexican accounts is filled with contradictions. For example, scholar Todd E. Harburn points out, "There are just too many significant variations in the number of those executed [in] these accounts." These numbers range from one to seven, including almost every number in between. "It is very suspect that these officers would not have a more closely corresponding count of those involved if they had truly witnessed the event."[70]

Another problem cited by the doubters is the fact that the various Mexican accounts were sure Crockett was among the survivors. Yet none of the officers involved had ever met him. Moreover, his physical description varied widely in the different accounts, from a slow-moving old man to a vigorous young warrior.

Finally there was the testimony of San Antonio's *alcalde*, or local administrator, Francisco Antonio Ruiz. Because he had lent his support to the Texian cause, when the Mexican army had entered the town, Santa Anna had placed him under house arrest. Now that the Alamo had been captured, the dictator remembered that Ruiz knew Travis, Bowie, and Crockett fairly well. Ruiz said later:

Davy Crockett fights to the last in this painting. However, several Mexican officers later said Crockett was captured and executed by Santa Anna. The truth will probably never be known.

Santa Anna sent one of his aides with an order for [me] to come before him. He directed me to . . . accompany him, as he was desirous to have Colonels Travis, Bowie and Crockett shown to him. On the north battery of the fortress lay the lifeless body of Colonel Travis on the gun carriage shot only in the forehead. Toward the west in a small fort [enclosed space within a barricade] we found the body of Colonel Crockett.[71]

This recollection clearly does not jibe with the claim that Crockett survived the battle and came face-to-face with Santa Anna. If the latter had ordered and watched the frontiersman's execution, Harburn points out, "there would be no need for him to be shown, and have identified, Crockett's body." Of course, it is possible that de la Peña's account is the authentic one and that Ruiz fabricated parts of his own. So for the present, no resolution of the argument is in sight. "Until new evidence is discovered, and/or the de la Peña narrative is refuted or authenticated," Harburn writes, "the Crockett death controversy will likely continue."[72]

The Highest Life of All

In whatever manner Crockett actually died, the Battle of the Alamo was over by the time the sun had risen fully above the eastern horizon. All of the fort's more than 180 active defenders lay dead. (Joe and a handful of women and children were spared.) Yet these fighters had made Santa Anna pay a terrible price for his win. Most modern Alamo experts estimate that four hundred to six hundred Mexicans died in the final battle. "These were the flower of [the] army," Ruiz wrote. "The gallantry of the few Texians who defended the Alamo [was] really wondered at by the Mexican army. Even the generals were astonished at their vigorous resistance, and how dearly the victory had been bought."[73]

Nevertheless, Santa Anna had no intention of giving the enemy soldiers their due. In a letter to one of his leading supporters in Mexico City, he bragged, "Victory belongs to the army, which at this very moment, 8 o'clock

The First Newspaper Story of the Tragedy

The first newspaper story about the Alamo's fall was published on March 24, 1836, in the Telegraph and Texas Register. *The paper mainly used the account of Susannah Dickenson, wife of one of the defenders, although it was somewhat questionable because she was in an enclosed chamber during most of the attack and saw very little of it.*

At daybreak ... the enemy surrounded the fort with their infantry, with the cavalry forming a circle outside to prevent escape on the part of the garrison. General Santa Anna commanded in person, assisted by four generals and a formidable train of artillery. Our men had been previously much fatigued and harassed by night-watching and incessant toil, having experienced for some days past a heavy bombardment and several real and feigned attacks. . . . (T)wice did the enemy apply to the walls with their scaling ladders, and twice did they receive a check; for our men were determined to verify the words of the immortal Travis, "to make the victory worse to the enemy than a defeat."

Quoted in *Inside the Gates* (blog), Daughters of the Republic of Texas Library. "Newspaper Accounts of the Battle of the Alamo." http://drtlibrary.wordpress.com/2009/03/11/newspaper-accounts-of-the-battle-of-the-alamo.

A.M., achieved a complete and glorious triumph that will render its memory imperishable." The dictator then padded the numbers of enemy dead, saying that "600 corpses of foreigners" were found. He also grossly played down the number of Mexican casualties. "We lost about 70 men killed and 300 wounded,"[74] he lied.

In addition, for reasons only he knew, Santa Anna refused the Texians a proper burial. Instead, his soldiers stripped the bodies, callously piled them together, and burned them. Ruiz played a key role in this procedure. He later recalled that Santa Anna "ordered wood to be brought to burn the bodies of the Texians. He sent a company of [soldiers] with me to bring wood and dry branches from the neighboring forests."[75]

As the smoke that comprised what was left of the Texians' bodies drifted upward into the morning sky, most of the Mexican dead were buried in the local cemetery. Saddened by the loss of many countrymen, an aide to General Cos, José Juan Sánchez Navarro, wanted to create a memorial to them. An amateur poet, he composed a moving ode, saying in part that the fallen "are now in Heaven, to be blest for deeds that time cannot abate. They put their manhood to the test, and fearlessly they met their fate," for they were true patriots, and "a patriot's fall leads to the highest life of all."[76] It remains unknown whether Navarro realized his words were no less fitting a tribute to the Alamo's defenders than they were to those who had given their lives to capture it.

Chapter Six

The Alamo's Aftermath and Legacy

The siege and fall of the Alamo had two major legacies, one of them immediate, the other long lasting and still with us. In the immediate aftermath, the fort's slain defenders were viewed as martyrs to the ongoing Texian struggle for independence from Mexico. The phrase "Remember the Alamo!" became an instant rallying cry for those who carried on and won the fight against Santa Anna.

In the battle's long-term legacy, the Alamo became more broadly symbolic. It not only stood for Texas's sovereignty and liberty, but still stands more broadly for American freedom and even for universal *human* freedom. "That event, so lamentable and yet so glorious," a Texas newspaper stated after the battle, "is of such deep interest and excites so much our feelings that we shall never cease to celebrate it."[77] Indeed, the events surrounding the Alamo siege have become the stuff of legend, and close to two

centuries after the fact, they continue to inspire history buffs, novelists, painters, musicians, and especially filmmakers.

The Goliad Massacre

News of the Alamo's fall reached Sam Houston and most other Texian leaders four days later, on March 10, 1836. Realizing that Santa Anna would likely march on Goliad next, Houston swiftly fired off a message to warn James Fannin and urge him to evacuate his position. Fannin got the message and began to prepare his garrison for an orderly strategic retreat. But he also wasted precious days trying to convince the local settlers to leave, so by the time he and his men departed Goliad on March 19, it was too late. Fewer than two hours later, they were overtaken and surrounded by fifteen hundred Mexican soldiers under General José de Urrea.

There followed a small but ferocious pitched battle in an open field near Coleto Creek. When Urrea finally pulled his troops back to regroup them, nine Texians had been killed and about sixty wounded, including Fannin. The latter now concluded that the situation was hopeless. Worried that if the fight continued all of his men might die, as the Alamo defenders had, Fannin was relieved when he received a note from Urrea. It said, "If you gentlemen wish to surrender at discretion, the matter is ended. Otherwise I shall return to my camp and renew the attack."[78] In the negotiations that followed, Fannin agreed to surrender, and in exchange Urrea promised that the Texians would be treated as prisoners of war. Also, the wounded prisoners would receive medical treatment.

On March 20, per Urrea's order, the prisoners were locked up in a chapel in Goliad. The general then wrote to Santa

On March 27, 1836, at Goliad, Santa Anna ordered some four hundred Texians massacred. The Texians would not forget and would exact revenge at San Jacinto less than a month later.

Anna, urging clemency for Fannin and the others, and departed, leaving Lieutenant Colonel Nicolás de la Portilla in charge. A few days later Santa Anna replied to Urrea with a demand that the prisoners be killed without delay. The dictator also sent a similar command to Portilla, who was expected to carry out the executions.

Both Urrea and Portilla despaired over what they viewed as an unethical, inhumane order. Portilla later recalled how he "spent a restless night"[79] filled with anguish at being forced to slaughter prisoners in cold blood. But like so many other Mexican officers, he had little doubt that Santa Anna would execute him, too, if he disobeyed the order.

Thus, on March 27, 1836, a large number of armed soldiers marched an estimated 360 Texians out into a field and opened fire on them at nearly point blank range. In the midst of the smoke from the firing of massed muskets and the writhing of men in their death agonies, around twenty-eight of the prisoners managed to escape. Among them was Herman Ehrenberg, who later wrote an account of the massacre.

While this horror was unfolding, around forty of the wounded Texians who were still held prisoner in Goliad were slain in a similar manner. Fannin was killed separately while sitting in a chair, because the leg injury he had sustained at Coleto Creek made it too hard for him to stand. Fortunately for

Urrea's Regret over the Goliad Massacre

In his diary, General José de Urrea recalled his distress over Santa Anna's orders to "butcher" Fannin and the other prisoners at Goliad.

These orders always seemed to me harsh. . . . That massacre [was] a deed [forbidden] by the laws of war and condemned by the civilization [of] our country. It was painful to me, also, that so many brave men should thus be sacrificed, particularly the much esteemed and fearless [James] Fannin. They doubtlessly surrendered confident that Mexican generosity would not make their surrender useless. . . . I used my influence with the general-in-chief [Santa Anna] to save them, if possible, from being butchered, particularly Fannin. [But] I obtained from His Excellency only a severe reply, repeating his previous order [to brand all armed Texians pirates and kill them].

Quoted in Wallace L. McKeehan, ed. "Goliad Massacre Index." Sons of Dewitt Colony Texas. www.tamu.edu/faculty/ccbn/dewitt/goliadurrea.htm.

twenty other Texians in this group, they were saved by Francita Alavez, wife of a Mexican colonel, Telesforo Alavez. For hiding these men from the firing squads at the risk of her own life, later grateful Texas citizens came to call her the "Angel of Goliad."

Total Victory

Like most other residents of Texas, Sam Houston was saddened and disgusted by the news of the mass executions at Goliad. He was also a skilled military leader who knew he could use the Alamo and Goliad tragedies to further inflate anti-Mexican sentiment among Texians and Americans alike. He called on them to remember the men who had given their lives in the cause of liberty for Texas. This helped to swell the ranks of his army, which was soon eight hundred strong and still growing.

Meanwhile, Santa Anna had heard that in spite of the Texians' crippling losses at San Antonio and Goliad, some of them still insisted on carrying on the revolution. Hoping to crush the movement's last remnants, on April 14 the dictator took about 750 men and hurried to Harrisburg, lying east of the Brazos River. There he expected to capture the president of the infant Texian republic, David G. Burnet, and the members of his cabinet. But Burnet and the others were able to flee in the nick of time. Disappointed, Santa Anna then went looking for Houston, who was purported to be nearby.

By now Houston had more than nine hundred men. Adopting a cautious strategy, he avoided contact with the enemy until April 20. At that time the two armies were camped about 3,000 feet (915m) apart near the San Jacinto River, several miles south of Harrisburg. There, General Cos reinforced Santa Anna, whose men now numbered almost fifteen hundred. The dictator, as usual arrogant and overconfident, was certain that the far fewer Texians would not dare to attack his camp. So he protected it with only a waist-high breastwork (mound of earth) and posted few sentries.

This was a fatal mistake and an opportunity on which Houston promptly seized. At three thirty or four o'clock in the afternoon on April 21, 1836, most of the Mexicans were taking their usual afternoon siesta. In contrast to the calmness of that scene, the far side of the "no man's land" separating them from the enemy was suddenly alive with movement. Masses of mounted Texians burst "quickly out of the woods," as one modern expert describes it.

Silently and tensely the Texas battle line swept across the prairie [until it was] at close range. [Then the] men sprang forward . . . yelling, "Remember the Alamo!" [and] "Remember Goliad!" All together they opened fire, blazing away practically point-blank at the surprised and panic-stricken Mexicans. They stormed over the breastwork, seized the enemy's artillery, and joined in hand-to-hand combat, emptying their pistols, swinging

"We Must Now Act"

Thomas J. Rusk, the secretary of war of the new Republic of Texas, accompanied Sam Houston and his soldiers as they shadowed Santa Anna's army. Preparing for a major clash with the enemy, on April 19, 1836, the two leaders issued a final plea for Texian settlers to join their ranks. "Fellow-Citizens," Rusk exclaimed, "Let me make one more appeal to you to turn out and rally to the standard of your country." He urged them to "rise up at once" and "march to the field!" If they made "a vigorous effort," Texas would be safe and free. "What is life worth with the loss of liberty?"[1] he asked. In a dramatic flourish, Houston added, "We view ourselves on the eve of battle. We are nerved for the contest, and must conquer or perish. It is vain to look for present aid, [for] none is at hand. We must now act or abandon all hope! Rally to the standard, and be . . . free men, that your children may bless their father's name!"[2]

1. Quoted in Paul McWhorter. "The Battle of San Jacinto." www.sonofthesouth.net/texas/battle-san-jacinto .htm.
2. Quoted in McWhorter. "The Battle of San Jacinto."

their guns as clubs, [and] slashing right and left with their knives. Mexicans fell by the scores under the impact of the savage assault.[80]

Most of the surviving Mexicans wasted little time in surrendering.

The Battle of San Jacinto, as it came to be called, had lasted just eighteen minutes, but the casualty lists revealed the totality of the Texian victory. The Mexicans had lost 630 killed, 208 wounded, and 730 captured; the other side had only 9 dead and 30 wounded. Santa Anna escaped during the turmoil of battle. But some Texians found him the next day hiding in a stand of tall grass and brought him to General Houston. The two leaders talked for more than two hours, during which the Mexican president agreed to withdraw all of his troops from Texas and never return. "Thus ended the revolution of 1836," researcher Wallace L. McKeehan states. That brief battle "established Texas as a free republic and opened the way for the United States to extend its boundaries to the Rio Grande on the southwest and to the Pacific [Ocean] on the west. Few military engagements in history have been more decisive or of more far-reaching ultimate influence than the battle of San Jacinto."[81]

From Eyesore to Shrine

McKeehan's mention of the United States reflects the fact that the Republic of Texas existed as an independent nation only briefly. From its inception in 1836, the idea of making the territory part of the United States was widely popular among both Texians and Americans. (The term *Texian* remained in use until around 1850, after which *Texan* steadily replaced it.) A political movement for statehood gained steam in the early 1840s, and in December 1845 Texas became the twenty-eighth U.S. state.

From that time forward, the ultimate sacrifice made by the Alamo defenders became a proud piece of American heritage and lore, celebrated in historical writings, poems, and songs. Yet curiously, the actual building (more accurately a group of buildings) in which those heroes had perished was at first not seen

Sam Houston led the Texians in the destruction of Santa Anna's army in a mere eighteen minutes at the battle of San Jacinto on April 22, 1836.

A captured Santa Anna, disguised in a private's uniform, stands next to a reposing Sam Houston. Houston gave Santa Anna a choice: Texas independence or hanging; he chose the former.

as anything special. Indeed, in the late 1830s and into the 1840s, it was allowed to deteriorate and steadily crumbled. In 1849 the U.S. Army used what was left of the compound as a storage facility, and by the 1870s a wooden grocery store had been erected atop part of the ruins. In the 1880s a visitor expressed "amazement and disgust" that a monument to "the annals of liberty" was "filled with sacks of salt, stinking potatoes," and "odorous kerosene."[82]

This sad situation began to change with the establishment of the Daughters of the Republic of Texas (DRT) in 1892. The organization, dedicated to preserving historic Texan monuments, drew attention to the Alamo's remains and raised money to refurbish them. Thanks to such efforts, the Alamo became a U.S. National Historic Landmark in 1960.

Today the Alamo consists of two of the original buildings—the chapel and long barracks (now a museum)—and a landscaped area beside them. There is also a gift shop and the DRT Research Library, built in 1950. No longer a forgotten, crumbling eyesore, the Alamo is a shrine and Texas's most popular tourist spot. Say Randy Roberts and James S. Olson:

Millions of people visit the place where Travis, Bowie, Crockett, and the others perished. Most of the visitors stand silent, or shuffle about slowly and quietly, as if for once in their lives they are on ground [equal in size] to their reverence. Other visitors wander about with looks of scorn,

A Marketing Bonanza

Walt Disney's television shows depicting Davy Crockett's adventures were so popular that Disney enjoyed a marketing bonanza of epic proportions, described here by historians Randy Roberts and James S. Olson.

Practically overnight, in a miracle of capitalism, everything that had to do with Davy Crockett [was] for sale with his name attached. . . . Any American boy with enough money or willing parents could wear a buckskin Davy Crockett jacket, cotton Davy Crockett shirt, denim Davy Crockett pants, and stylish Davy Crockett underwear. He could carry a wood or plastic Davy Crockett rifle and load it with a Davy Crockett powder horn. . . . After several hair-raising adventures, he could go home to a meal served on Davy Crockett plates, drink milk from a Davy Crockett mug, bathe with Davy Crockett soap, dry off with a Davy Crockett towel, slip into a pair of Davy Crockett pajamas [and] go to bed between Davy Crockett sheets. [There were also Davy Crockett] T-shirts, raincoats . . . bicycles, tricycles, face powder, ropes, jigsaw puzzles, ice cream cups, athletic equipment . . . toy logs, dart games, books, trucks, wagons, board games, rings, and on and on.

Randy Roberts and James S. Olson. *A Line in the Sand: The Alamo in Blood and Memory.* New York: Simon and Schuster, 2002, pp. 243–244.

sure that there is nothing sacred or even noble about the Alamo shrine. For all visitors, the Alamo is both history and memory, as alive today as it was in the nineteenth century.[83]

Molding the Legend

Except for the shrine itself, nowhere else do the Alamo's history and memory remain more alive in the public mind than in the many films that have been made about the 1836 siege. These movies, film historian Frank Thompson explains, "have molded the endlessly pliable legend to accommodate changing perceptions and needs. Future films will do it again," as they tell and retell "this great story for generations of Texans and Americans."[84]

The famous 1955 Walt Disney version and 1960 John Wayne adaptation were only a small part of this cultural phenomenon. Beginning with *The Immortal Alamo*, a 1911 silent film, almost a dozen major theatrical and TV versions portrayed the battle and the events leading up to it. Particularly notable were *The Last Command* (1955), *The Alamo: Thirteen Days to Glory* (1987), and *The Alamo* (2004). The latter, with Billy Bob Thornton as Davy Crocket, was arguably the most historically accurate version.

The Alamo's defenders are immortalized in stone at the Cenotaph memorial in San Antonio. For Texans the Alamo is both history and legend.

sion. (However, some scholars and Alamo buffs were unhappy about the filmmakers' choice to dramatize the narrative of José Enrique de la Peña and show Crockett temporarily survive the battle.)

In addition, dozens of movies and TV shows have dealt with the Alamo and its fall briefly or in passing. *Man of Conquest* (1939), a bio-epic about Sam Houston, is an example. Another is *The Man from the Alamo* (1953), a fictional tale of a settler who left the fort shortly before its fall and went on to save many other settlers from brutality and injustice. A number of Alamo documentaries have been made as well. One of the best was Brian Huberman's 1991 production *The Making of John Wayne's "The Alamo."*

Where History and Mythology Blur

Some experts have called attention to a drawback of the films' constant reshaping of the Alamo story for dramatic effect. Namely, this frequently makes it difficult for nonscholars to separate the facts from the legends. Indeed, a popular Alamo book points out, in the public mind the Alamo battle is in large degree "a place where fact [and] fable [blend] and the boundaries between history and mythology blur."[85] In that special place of imagination, what Travis, Crockett, and the other heroes actually said and how they really died is not paramount. Often more important is how individual viewers feel the events *could* or *should* have occurred.

Still, no myths, fabrications, or dramatized film reenactments can quite replicate the horror and grandeur of the real battle. Nor can they capture the bravery and heroism of those who fought it—Texians and Mexicans alike. They were not mythic characters back then, on that cold, dark morning in March, says Stephen L. Hardin, but rather "flesh-and-blood human beings." Considering that,

they were even more heroic. [The] soldiers on both sides of the walls were individuals far from home, stuck with an unpleasant job, and fervently wishing they were somewhere else. Even so, when one strips away the layers of myth . . . what is left is still grandly heroic. The Alamo remains a shining moment in Texas history. Those Texians and what they accomplished do not require fabrication to remind us of their legacy. For ultimately, the heroism endures.[86]

Notes

Introduction: The Alamo in the Public Mind

1. Randy Roberts and James S. Olson. *A Line in the Sand: The Alamo in Blood and Memory*. New York: Simon and Schuster, 2002, p. vii.
2. Michael Wallis. *David Crockett: The Lion of the West*. New York: Norton, 2011, p. xiii.
3. Quoted in IMDb. "Memorable Quotes for *The Alamo* (1960)." www.imdb.com/title/tt0053580/quotes.
4. Quoted in Donald Clark and Christopher P. Andersen. *John Wayne's "The Alamo": The Making of the Epic Film*. New York: Citadel, 1995, p. 105.
5. Quoted in Alan C. Huffines. *Blood of Noble Men: The Alamo Siege and Battle*. Austin, TX: Eakin, 2006, p. viii.
6. Huffines. *Blood of Noble Men*, p. xi.

Chapter One: Anglos Overrun the Texas Frontier

7. Edwin P. Hoyt. *The Alamo: An Illustrated History*. Dallas: Taylor Trade, 2003, p. i.
8. Irwin Unger. *These United States: The Questions of Our Past*. Vol. 1. Upper Saddle River, NJ: Pearson, 2007, p. 248.
9. Quoted in Hoyt. *The Alamo*, p. 11.
10. Tim J. Todish and Terry S. Todish. *Alamo Sourcebook, 1836: A Compre-hensive Guide to the Alamo and the Texas Revolution*. Austin, TX: Eakin, 1998, p. 3.
11. Quoted in Cecil Robinson, ed. and trans. *The View from Chapultepec: Mexican Writers on the Mexican-American War*. Tucson: University of Arizona Press, 1989, pp. xxix–xxx.
12. Todish and Todish. *Alamo Sourcebook*, p. 3.
13. Quoted in Spartacus Educational. "Stephen Austin." www.spartacus.schoolnet.co.uk/WWaustin.htm.
14. Roberts and Olson. *A Line in the Sand*, p. 35.
15. Quoted in Texas State Library and Archives Commission. "Turtle Bayou Resolutions." www.tsl.state.tx.us/treasures/republic/turtle/turtle-1.html.
16. Quoted in Roberts and Olson. *A Line in the Sand*, p. 51.
17. Quoted in Amelia W. Williams. *The Alamo Defenders: A Critical Study of the Siege of the Alamo and the Personnel of Its Defenders*. Ingleside, TX: Copano Bay, 2010, p. 56.
18. Quoted in Gene M. Brack. *Mexico Views Manifest Destiny, 1821–1846*. Albuquerque: University of New Mexico Press, 1975, p. 96.
19. Quoted in T.R. Fehrenbach. *Lone Star: A History of Texas and Texans*. New York: Da Capo, 2000, p. 152.

Chapter Two: Bloodshed Sparks Open Rebellion

20. Quoted in Robinson. *The View from Chapultepec*, pp. 59–61.
21. Quoted in Todd Hansen, ed. *The Alamo Reader: A Study in History*. Mechanicsburg, PA: Stackpole, 2003, pp. 9–10.
22. Quoted in Wallace L. McKeehan, ed. "The Battle of Gonzales." Sons of Dewitt Colony Texas. www.tamu .edu/faculty/ccbn/dewitt/batgon taylor.htm.
23. Quoted in José C. Valdes. *Mexico, Santa Anna, and the War for Texas*. Mexico City: Editorial Diana, 1993, p. 97.
24. Jeff Long. *Duel of Eagles: The Mexican and U.S. Fight for the Alamo*. New York: William Morrow, 1990, p. 91.
25. T.R. Fehrenbach. *Fire and Blood: A History of Mexico*. New York: Da Capo, 1995, p. 373.
26. Long, *Duel of Eagles*, pp. 96–97.
27. Quoted in Paul McWhorter. "First Revolutionary Movement in Texas, 1834–1835." www.sonofthesouth .net/texas/first-revolutionary -movement.htm.
28. Quoted in Texas State Library and Archives Commission. "Stephen F. Austin to James Bowie and James Fannin, November 1, 1835." www .tsl.state.tx.us/treasures/republic /bexar/austin-bowie-1.html.
29. Quoted in Texas State Library and Archives Commission. "The Siege of Bexar: From the Republic Pension Application of Joseph Lopez." www.tsl.state.tx.us/treasures /republic/bexar/lopez.html.
30. Quoted in Roberts and Olson. *A Line in the Sand*, p. 59.
31. Quoted in Alwyn Barr. *Texas in Revolt*. Austin: University of Texas Press, 1991, p. 57.

Chapter Three: Santa Anna's Army Invades Texas

32. Quoted in Todish and Todish. *Alamo Sourcebook*, p. 14.
33. Quoted in Archives of *The West*. "Declaration of the People of Texas." PBS. www.pbs.org/weta /thewest/resources/archives/two /texdec.htm.
34. Quoted in Hansen. *The Alamo Reader*, p. 19.
35. Quoted in Roberts and Olson. *A Line in the Sand*, p. 112.
36. Quoted in Williams. *The Alamo Defenders*, p. 45.
37. Quoted in Texas State Historical Association. "James Bowie." www .tshaonline.org/handbook/online /articles/fbo45.
38. Quoted in Texian Legacy Association. "David Crockett's Letter to His Children." www.texianlegacy .com/crockettletter.html.
39. William C. Davis. *Three Roads to the Alamo*. New York: HarperCollins, 1999, p. 539.
40. Quoted in Texas State Historical Association. "Battle of the Alamo." www.tshaonline.org/handbook /online/articles/qea02.

Chapter Four: The Alamo Is Surrounded and Besieged

41. Quoted in Timothy M. Matovina. *The Alamo Remembered: Tejano Accounts and Perspectives*. Austin: University of Texas Press, 1995, pp. 93–94.
42. Quoted in Huffines. *Blood of Noble Men*, p. 24.

43. Quoted in Matovina. *The Alamo Remembered*, p. 74.

44. Quoted in Wallace O. Chariton. *100 Days in Texas: The Alamo Letters.* Plano, TX: Wordware, 1989, p. 263.

45. Quoted in Digital History. "Antonio Lopez de Santa Anna, February 27, 1836." www.digitalhistory.uh.edu/learning_history/alamo/preparing4.cfm.

46. Quoted in Hansen. *The Alamo Reader*, p. 32.

47. Quoted in James T. De Shields. *Tall Men with Long Rifles: The Glamorous Story of the Texas Revolution as Told by Captain Creed Taylor.* San Antonio, TX: Naylor, 1915, p. 163.

48. Quoted in Huffines. *Blood of Noble Men*, p. 54.

49. Quoted in Davis. *Three Roads to the Alamo*, p. 542.

50. Quoted in Howard R. Driggs and Sarah S. King. *Rise of the Lone Star: A Story of Texas Told by Its Pioneers.* New York: Frederick A. Stokes, 1936, pp. 220–221.

51. Todish and Todish. *Alamo Sourcebook*, p. 46.

52. Quoted in Avalon Project. "The Texas Declaration of Independence, March 2, 1836." http://avalon.law.yale.edu/19th_century/texdec.asp.

53. Quoted in Digital History. "William Barret Travis, March 3, 1836." www.digitalhistory.uh.edu/learning_history/alamo/preparing6.cfm.

Chapter Five: The Final Assault and the Alamo's Fall

54. Quoted in Digital History. "Fernando Urizza (Mexican Colonel), 1859." www.digitalhistory.uh.edu/learning_history/alamo/following9.cfm.

55. Quoted in Digital History. "Manuel Loranca (Mexican Sergeant), June 23, 1878." www.digitalhistory.uh.edu/learning_history/alamo/following11.cfm.

56. Quoted in Digital History. "Unidentified Mexican Soldier, April 5, 1836." www.digitalhistory.uh.edu/learning_history/alamo/following1.cfm.

57. Quoted in Digital History. "Unidentified Mexican Soldier, April 5, 1836."

58. Quoted in *American Experience.* "Remember the Alamo: Survival Stories." PBS. www.pbs.org/wgbh/amex/alamo/sfeature/sf_survivors.html.

59. Hoyt. *The Alamo*, p. 105.

60. Quoted in *American Experience.* "Remember the Alamo."

61. Quoted in *American Experience.* "Remember the Alamo."

62. Todish and Todish. *Alamo Sourcebook*, p. 52.

63. Quoted in EyeWitness to History. "'Remember the Alamo!,' 1836." www.eyewitnesstohistory.com/alamo.htm.

64. Quoted in Digital History. "Manuel Loranca (Mexican Sergeant), June 23, 1878."

65. Quoted in EyeWitness to History. "'Remember the Alamo!' 1836."

66. Quoted in Roberts and Olson. *A Line in the Sand*, p. 166.

67. Quoted in *American Experience.* "Remember the Alamo."

68. Quoted in Huffines, *Blood of Noble Men*, p. 181.

69. Quoted in Huffines. *Blood of Noble Men*, p. 181.
70. Quoted in Todish and Todish. *Alamo Sourcebook*, p. 99.
71. Quoted in Alamo de Parras. "The Story of the Fall of the Alamo." www.tamu.edu/faculty/ccbn/dewitt/adp/archives/newsarch/ruizart.html.
72. Quoted in Todish and Todish. *Alamo Sourcebook*, pp. 99–100.
73. Quoted in Alamo de Parras. "The Story of the Fall of the Alamo."
74. Quoted in Chariton. *100 Days in Texas*, p. 324.
75. Quoted in Alamo de Parras. "The Story of the Fall of the Alamo."
76. Quoted in Huffines. *Blood of Noble Men*, p. 206.

Chapter Six: The Alamo's Aftermath and Legacy

77. Quoted in Hansen. *The Alamo Reader*, p. 551.
78. Quoted in Wallace L. McKeehan, ed. "Goliad Massacre Index." Sons of DeWitt Colony Texas. www.tamu.edu/faculty/ccbn/dewitt/goliadurrea.htm.
79. Quoted in McKeehan. "Goliad Massacre Index."
80. Quoted in Wallace L. McKeehan, ed. "The Battle of San Jacinto." Sons of DeWitt Colony Texas. www.tamu.edu/faculty/ccbn/dewitt/batsanjacinto.htm.
81. McKeehan. "The Battle of San Jacinto."
82. Quoted in Roberts and Olson. *A Line in the Sand*, p. 202.
83. Roberts and Olson. *A Line in the Sand*, p. vii.
84. Frank Thompson. *Alamo Movies*. East Berlin, PA: Old Mill, 1991, pp. 15–16.
85. Roberts and Olson. *A Line in the Sand*, p. 348.
86. Quoted in Huffines. *Blood of Noble Men*, p. viii.

For More Information

Books

William C. Binkley, ed. *Official Correspondence of the Texas Revolution, 1835–1836.* 2 vols. New York: D. Appleton, 1938. A valuable collection of letters and other documents related to the anti-Mexican rebellion that led to the fall of the Alamo and independence for Texas.

Donald Clark and Christopher P. Andersen. *John Wayne's "The Alamo": The Making of the Epic Film.* New York: Citadel, 1995. Although Wayne's famous epic is long and ponderous, the final battle scenes are spectacular, and this entertaining book tells how they were created, as well as sheds light, through comparisons, on the real Alamo siege and battle.

William C. Davis. *Three Roads to the Alamo.* New York: HarperCollins, 1999. A long, well-researched account of how three men—Davy Crockett, Jim Bowie, and William Barret Travis—ended up at the Alamo and heroically died there.

Stephen L. Hardin. *Texian Iliad: A Military History of the Texas Revolution.* Austin: University of Texas Press, 1996. Hardin delivers a painstakingly researched, masterfully written examination of the events leading up to the Alamo's fall, along with the battle itself.

Edwin P. Hoyt. *The Alamo: An Illustrated History.* Dallas: Taylor Trade, 2003. This is an accurate, very easy-to-read overview that people with no prior background in the subject will find very useful.

Alan C. Huffines. *Blood of Noble Men: The Alamo Siege and Battle.* Austin, TX: Eakin, 2006. This superb book by a retired military officer and gifted historian is widely viewed as one of the two best studies of the Alamo battle currently available.

Annie Jane Leavitt. *The Alamo: An Interactive History Adventure.* Mankato, MN: Capstone, 2007. Aimed at younger readers, this nicely mounted, appealing volume allows the reader to follow different historical paths, each of which presents the events of the Texas Revolution from a different point of view.

Jim Murphy. *Inside the Alamo.* New York: Delacorte, 2003. Thoroughly researched and extremely well written, this is one of the best tellings of the Alamo and its surrounding events written for young adults. Ambitious grade-school readers will enjoy and benefit from it, too.

Randy Roberts and James S. Olson. *A Line in the Sand: The Alamo in Blood and Memory.* New York: Simon and Schuster, 2002. This well-written volume first describes the Texas Revolution and Alamo battle, and then explores their extensive cultural legacy in considerable detail.

Antonio López de Santa Anna. *The Eagle: The Autobiography of Santa Anna*. Edited by Ann F. Crawford. Translated by Sam Guyler and Jaime Platon. Austin, TX: Pemberton, 1967. Santa Anna's description of his own pompous goals and deeds is slanted but still an important historical document in its own right.

Lon Tinkle. *Thirteen Days to Glory*. College Station: Texas A&M University Press, 1996. Movingly written, this is one of the better existing studies of the Alamo's story.

Tim J. Todish and Terry S. Todish. *Alamo Sourcebook, 1836: A Comprehensive Guide to the Alamo and the Texas Revolution*. Austin, TX: Eakin, 1998. Along with Alan C. Huffines's book (see above), this impressive, absorbing, and easy to follow piece of scholarship is widely seen as one of the two most valuable volumes on the Alamo.

Michael Wallis. *David Crockett: The Lion of the West*. New York: Norton, 2011. A rollicking, accurate study of the well-known frontiersman, the book keeps his mythical qualities intact yet also manages to capture most of the real events of his life.

Gary S. Zaboly. *An Altar for Their Sons: The Alamo and the Texas Revolution in Contemporary Newspaper Accounts*. Buffalo Gap, TX: State House, 2011. Zaboly, who illustrated Alan Huffines's classic Alamo book (see above), has done a fine job of editing a wide range of Alamo-related materials, including newspaper articles, essays, poems, photos, and some new illustrations of his own. Young people and adults alike will find the collection fascinating.

Websites

Alamo (http://thealamo.org). The official site of the Alamo, this contains links to the shrine, museum, gift shop, historical accounts, and other helpful information about the Alamo.

Alton S. Tobey's Painting of "The Battle at the Alamo" (http://the-alamo-san-antonio.com/tobey-painting.htm). A handsome color shot of the late, noted historical illustrator Alton S. Tobey's famous 1963 painting showing some of the Alamo defenders fighting to their deaths as they are swarmed by enemy soldiers.

Antonio López de Santa Anna, PBS (www.pbs.org/wgbh/amex/alamo/peopleevents/p_santaanna.html). Like its other online historical tracts, PBS's biography of the Mexican dictator is first-rate.

Battle of San Jacinto, Sons of DeWitt Colony Texas (www.tamu.edu/faculty/ccbn/dewitt/batsanjacinto.htm). An information-packed account of the battle and surrounding events.

The Battle of the Alamo (www.youtube.com/watch?v=HVBm3y_PMtY). This five-minute video presentation on YouTube blends still images, text, and music in an effective overview of the high points of the siege.

Battle of the Alamo, Texas State Historical Association (www.tshaonline

.org/handbook/online/articles/AA/qea2.html). This is part of a comprehensive and useful collection of short articles about the Alamo and the Texas Revolution compiled by the Texas State Historical Association.

Frequently Asked Questions About the Battle of the Alamo (www.jman5.com/alamo/frequently-asked-questions-about-the-alamo.htm#davy). This extremely valuable and fascinating site provides answers to questions that people studying about the Alamo commonly ask.

Goliad Massacre (www.sonofthesouth.net/texas/goliad-massacre.htm). This tells the tragic story of the more than three hundred Texians who were taken prisoner shortly after the Alamo's fall and murdered in cold blood at Santa Anna's order.

John Wayne: *The Alamo*; **A Tribute Site** (http://johnwayne-thealamo.com/film_scenes.html). Click the button in the middle to see a slide show of dramatic highlights from Wayne's version of the siege.

Sam Houston (www.sonofthesouth.net/texas/sam-houston.htm). This short, easy-to-read biography of Houston contains links to other people and events surrounding the Alamo and Texas Revolution.

Stephen F. Austin, PBS (www.pbs.org/wgbh/amex/alamo/peopleevents/p_austin.html). This is a well-written, accurate biography of Austin and his achievements.

Texas, Texans, and the Alamo, University of Texas (www.cah.utexas.edu/exhibits/TexasExhibit/Texas1.html). By clicking on "Next Page" at the bottom, the viewer can find a number of photos of key places and documents pertaining to the Texas Revolution.

Index

San Jacinto, battle of (1836),
   81–82, *83*
Santa Anna, Antonio López de,
   10, *34, 57, 66*
   attack on Zacatecas by, 35
   capture of, *84*
   defeat of, at San Jacinto,
      81–82
   Goliad massacre and, 79–80
   orders disarming of militias,
      31
   orders final assault on the
      Alamo, 65–67
   as paradox, 34
   on punishment of Texians for
      seize of San Antonio, 39
   rise to power of, 32–33
   strategy of, 55–57
   on victory at the Alamo,
      76–77
Sesma, Joaquín Ramírez y, 40
Slavery, 22, 23–24
Smith, Henry, 44, 49
Smithwick, Noah, 43–44

T
Taylor, Creed, 32
Tejas, Anglo settlement of, 17–18,
   21, 22, *22*
Telegraph and Texas Register
   (newspaper), 76

Terán, Manuel de Mier y, 30
Texas
   Republic of, 63, 82–83
   statehood granted to, 83
Texas Declaration of
   Independence, *45*
Texas Rangers, forerunners of,
   21
Texas Revolution (1835–1836),
   31–32
   end of, 82
   inevitability of, 29–30
Texians (Anglo settlers), 21,
   22
   declare independent
      republic of Texas, 63
   encouragement of, 17–18
   flouting of Mexican law by,
      23–25
   Goliad massacre of, 78–81, *79*
   inevitability of war between
      Mexico and, 29–30
   magnets for, 22
   set up provisional
      government, 44
   state of military of, 40–44
Tolsa, Eugenio, 40
Travis, William Barret, *49*, 55,
   63, *63*
   assumes leadership of San
      Antonio forces, 49–50
   death of, 70
   "Victory or Death" statement
      of, *59*

Picture Credits

About the Author

In addition to his acclaimed volumes about the ancient world, historian and award-winning author Don Nardo has published numerous books for young people about American history. They include overviews of America's wars, studies of the U.S. founders and their timeless documents, and examinations of the history and culture of the Native Americans. Nardo also composes and arranges orchestral music. He lives with his wife, Christine, in Massachusetts.